YOU ARE A DAMN POWERHOUSE

YOU ARE A DAMN POWERHOUSE

9 POWERFUL SECRETS TO (RE)DISCOVERING YOUR INNER-STRENGTH AND TRANSFORMING PAST PAIN INTO PURPOSE

REBECCA MUTETE

DISCLAIMER

This book is not intended as a substitute for the medical advice of physicians. The reader should regularly consult a physician in matters relating to his/her health and particularly with respect to any symptoms that may require diagnosis or medical attention.

CONTENTS

TESTIMONIALS

Wow! I couldn't stop reading. This book had me on the edge of my seat. I felt excited, sad, inspired, and more. This book is a must-have. We have to learn to push through life knowing all things will work for our good if we just believe. God sends his people for his people. It may only be for a moment, but it is necessary to get you to the next season of your life. Though tailored to women, men can also benefit by learning how women would like to be treated. Even as a daughter, sister, niece, aunt, or wife. I believe this will bless and benefit many on their journey in life.

Love Your Sister in Strength,

Rodrika Jones, founder & CEO of Pearl Woman, certified life coach, purpose strategist, and author of *My Choice of Words Changed My Life*

Travel and academics always connect me to vibrant personalities in this world, and Ms. Rebecca Mutete is among them. My days as a visiting scholar at St. Paul's College, Ottawa, paved the way for my connection with her. This book comes from real-life experiences where we find an unseen touch with our life as well. We can find a logical progression of life events in this book, and I am impressed with the way the author changed all her stumbling blocks in order to win her life.

Anish K. Joy, assistant professor in Christian anthropology and spirituality, research scholar at the Pontifical University Antonianum, visiting scholar at Saint Paul University, and guest lecturer at Dr. Engel Realschule, Germany.

Rebecca's story is full of adversities, strength, tenacity, gratitude, and hope. This story reminds of one thing -- you have to take part in your own rescue.

Koffi Aouga, senior marketing director, World Financial Group

You Are a Damn Powerhouse is a practical step-by-step guide that will help and inspire you to step into your purpose and achieve your wildest dreams. It's been a blessing and an honour knowing Rebecca and having her as a sister.

Romelle Sua, residential counsellor, Tamir Foundation

Don't take the title of this book lightly. Rebecca's story will be a voice to many young girls who feel disenfranchised or as if they have gotten the bitter end of the stick. It encourages them to rise beyond the pain and walk forward in trust that their past does not determine their destiny. For a lady who experienced brokenness, Rebecca has shared how she journeyed through her trauma to a point of finding inner-strength to propel her healing. Thank you for sharing your story, Rebecca; it was raw and riveting and a genuine expression of healing -- for the greatest hindrance to healing is silence.

Sania Dookie, MH therapist, JMT coach, speaker and trainer

You write it as it is, and I feel like many of my single-mom clients can benefit from it. It takes courage to share a personal story like yours, and you have done it with perfection. I love your braveness and sense of humour.

Dr. Narine Dat Sookram, Hon. DLitt, BSW, BPA-HS, SSW

DEDICATION

You are a Damn Powerhouse is dedicated to two phenomenal groups of people:

First, to my amazing children Hope, Barak, and Benny Mutete who have been, and continue to be, my motivators. I thank them for loving me unconditionally and reminding me daily of how amazing I am both as a person and as their mama. It's an indescribable feeling.

Second, I would like to dedicate this book to all of the wonderful, hardworking, ever-grinding single mamas out there who have found yourselves in a single parenting home by various means. While everyone's approach to single motherhood and life is different, I applaud you for walking your journey with grace and for taking this step forward – that of turning your pain and struggles into a testament.

I hope this book will stir your soul and remind you of your limitless potential. Most importantly, I hope this reminds you of the powerhouse nature within you. You have all you need to live a life of fulfilment and purpose. I wholeheartedly BELIEVE IN YOU! I will hold that belief for you until you can hold it for yourself.

ACKNOWLEDGMENTS

I would like to say a special thank you to those who have inspired and supported me into becoming the powerhouse I am today.

To my heavenly Father, the creator of Heaven and Earth, who works everything out for my own good, I thank you for strengthening me and enabling me to turn my trials into triumphs. I am not sure if I would have shared my testimony if it were not for your unconditional love and mercy for me.

My heartfelt appreciation, deep gratitude, and love to my best friend and sister who became my rock at the time I needed someone the most. My dearest Lissy Rosey, I owe you all the respect and love in the world, and I know there is nothing I can ever say or do to repay your unconditional love and kindness to me. You will never fully understand how much I love and appreciate you. You climbed the mountains with me; you became my family and a friend when I didn't have one; you tried your best to understand what I said with my rocky, limited English; and you spent many days and hours teaching me things about life and the beautiful Canadian culture.

Lissy, you took my displaced pieces of a puzzle and somewhat made it a full map without judging me as the pregnant runaway girl I was. You were with me through some of my ugliest relationships. You attended courts with me, ran after buses with me, and even after you fell down, you got up and did it all over again. You carried wood on your head like an African all the way to the hospital when I called you last minute to tell you I was heading to the hospital to get induced. I'll never forget how you were on your way from the hardware store, having bought material to fix things in my home, and you didn't care or worry about what other people thought about you carrying wood on your head to the massive Grand River Hospital.

You became my advisor, although half of the time I didn't listen. You became my helper, the fixer-of-things in my house, and an amazing auntie to my children. You took me home to your family, who graciously accepted me as one of their own and became my bonus (spiritual) family. You spent many days and months away from your home and other important things to help me after having my Benny boy, which is a story on its own. You housed me and my beautiful children in your home and didn't even ask for a penny (after I tried escaping the shame from my thirty days of marriage to a total stranger). You wrote many unpleasant emails on my behalf and edited many. My dearest, beautiful sis, no words can describe what you mean to me, but I pray day and night for your abundant blessings. May God grant you all your heart's desires in the mighty name of Jesus Christ who has blessed my womb.

I would love to take this moment to acknowledge and appreciate my beautiful mama Beatrice for bringing me into this world and for all the struggles, hate, and tribal discrimination she endured as a widow raising six children. Thank you for ensuring we got a fair shot at opportunities by doing everything within your means, and beyond, to bring us to Canada. Mummy, I may have questioned myself about many things, including your love for me, and even doubted if you were my mom for many years, and I may have hated you and resented you (please forgive me, I just didn't understand) for abandoning me, but I love you. Yes, we have had a rocky relationship on and off, but you remain my beloved mama, and I wouldn't trade you for the world. You are a true definition of strength, resilience, excellency, love, humility, generosity, and beauty. I thank God for you, I love you, I honour you, and I am forever grateful to you!

I would also like to take this opportunity to wholeheartedly appreciate my spiritual parents, Heather and Brian, for not only welcoming me and my children into their home as one of theirs, but for opening their hearts and welcoming me in without holding back. I can't thank you enough for all your love and devotion to myself, my children, and my family. Papa, thank you for being the best Pops to my children. Mama, thank you for believing in me. You were one of the reasons I believed I could write a book. You confirmed my admiration for expressing myself through writing when you said, "You express yourself so beautifully in your writing" after reading my post on Facebook. Thank you, Bamzi and Pops!

A huge thank you to Dr. Ava Eagle Brown who is another powerhouse of a single mama. Her mission is to see more women step into their purpose and amplify their voices. Ava, thank you so much for holding my hand through this journey, for believing in me, and for taking time to listen and understand my why, my passion, and my vision for my life and for this book. You rock!

Shout out to my phenomenal editor, Melanie Bright. Melanie, I just want to say thank you! I know that it wasn't necessarily easy to edit my work, but your professionalism, your attention to detail, your knowledge, and most importantly, your dedication and belief in my book did not go unnoticed. Thank you for going above and beyond editing. Thank you so much for being a part of this journey in the form of editing. You are a damn powerhouse!

A huge thank you to my two amazing families (biological and spiritual) and close friends at large for continuing to believe in me and support me with my wild dreams. I love and appreciate you all.

Last but not least, I want to thank the amazing women, from the bottom of my heart, who gave me a resounding YES when I reached out to ask if they would be open to sharing a bit of their life stories, and some words of wisdom, to bless and encourage other women. I admire their strength, their work, and I believe in their mission. A sincere thank you Glenda, Jennifer, Sabrina, and Betty!

PREFACE

Being a teen mom in a family of strong opinions, I felt alone, exhausted, and worthless. I'd left the father of my child behind and immigrated to Canada for greener pastures.

> The stress began the day you learned you were expected to please other people. Parents wanted you to stay clean and be quiet. Neighbours wanted you to be respectful and helpful. Teachers wanted you to be attentive and alert. Friends wanted you to share and hang out. Whenever you failed to do exactly what someone expected of you, you weren't good, or good enough. You were bad, weak, or dumb. Unfortunately, you began to believe it. Giving in to the demands, day by day, you lost a little more of yourself and your understanding of the truth. The truth is you are fine, just the way you are! Perfect in your imperfection! You are divine! Growing brighter and more brilliant each day, you can accept the truth of who you are. The next time you want to know who you are, what you are, or if something is the right thing to do, don't ask your neighbour— ask the power within... and pay attention to the response! The divine power within knows exactly who I Am!
>
> -Iyanla Vanzant, *Acts of Faith (pg. 9)*

Sistergirl, I know far too well what being brought down to a shell feels like. I was pregnant at sixteen, and I was trying to integrate into Canadian society. Instead of feeling the joy of bringing a life into the world, my family and the Immigration workers who were helping us settle into Canadian society, made me feel shameful, stupid, and useless. I took on emotional and physical beatings from my family who also restricted me from continuing with my education.

I was told that if I wanted to go to school, then I should have kept my legs closed. My family saw me like a slave whose job was only to cook and clean for people who "wanted" to go to school, which also included taking my little brother to and from school.

In addition to in-home slavery, my family restricted me from communicating with the father of my then unborn child, which took a toll on me emotionally. Nor could I open my mouth whenever I craved for something (like other pregnant women do) because I knew I would receive insults and be spat on instead.

In their eyes, I had dishonoured them and had brought shame by not continuing with my education and waiting for marriage to have sex. Instead, I got pregnant, which was unthinkable.

In African culture, it's a common belief that a good girl can bring honour to her family by completing her education (if the opportunity is available) and getting married before having children.

Girls are treated drastically better if the groom's family paid a dowry, also known as bride price (a "thank you for raising your daughter well" kind of thing), to the girl's family than if the groom paid nothing. For the brides whose groom paid a dowry, her soon-to-be husband is usually well-welcomed and respected at home by the bride's family. She is also cherished much more than if nothing was paid.

In my case, they believed me to be a disgrace to the family -- not only because there was no dowry, but I was pregnant so young, I didn't have a husband, and it was the worst time. I got pregnant at the time my family had been waiting for a lifetime opportunity (to come to Canada), which brought the worst out of them (caused by the fear of Immigration putting a hold on our ability to travel). Anytime a girl our family knew got married, and the groom had paid a dowry, my family would compare me to her. I endured insults from my mom of how other moms had good daughters while she wasted her time. It's almost as if my mom would mourn having me as a daughter.

At seven months pregnant, I decided it was time to speak up and break free. I confided in my translator from Healthy Babies Healthy Children who eventually helped me escape to a nearby abused women's shelter. Later, I was transferred to a young mom's shelter, and I lived there safely until after I gave birth.

The shameful words like, "You are useless. You are just here to cause pain and shame to the family. You are so stupid. Why did you open your legs if you wanted to go to school?" rang in my head on a daily basis, if not hourly.

I held on to those words for so long, and they kept ringing in my head until 2012 while I was home doing what I knew how to do best—watching TV.

A commercial popped up; it seemed almost like a sign from God. It probably wasn't the first time I had seen it because I saw it many more times after, but maybe it was the first time I paid attention to it. The commercial was of a single mom, like me, who went to college while raising her son. She talked about what it had done for her and her son financially. I'm not sure what happened that day, but it shot straight into my heart, and I am glad it did.

I can't tell you where my courage came from that day, but I knew this was all I needed to feel reassured that if she could do it as a single mom, then so could I. I packed up my children into a double stroller and headed for a bus on that rainy afternoon. From that day forward, I decided to let go of negative thoughts. It transformed my pain into confidence and self-trust, and I fell madly in love with myself -- inside and out. I began to realize my greatness.

Honey, may this book do for you what this commercial did for me that day!

I want every single mom who feels tired, who feels self-doubt, who has lost hope, or is just about to give up, to understand that you can turn your life around. A new life is readily available to you. Within you is a life free from resentment. You can enjoy pure self-love by letting go of the labels that no longer serve you in any way, shape, or form. These labels only drain you of life and your birthright to happiness. It's time to stop beating up yourself, and it's time to stop those sneaky negative thoughts, which block your ability to receive whatever the universe has to offer.

Writing this book has been a journey that has truly brought me so much joy, healing, and realization. It was filled with many tears, so much gratitude, and fulfilment, and my prayer is that it will bring you the same healing. I designed this book to demonstrate how you can show up powerfully in your own way, not in the way defined by the naysayers, opinionated family members, friends, or haters who imposed labels on you in order to dictate what you can or can't do.

Throughout the book, I will share some hardships I endured as a child, as a teen mom, and as an adult, including situations of abuse, rejection, loneliness, shame, negativity, and poor self-image. Likewise, I will share the powerful steps I used to overcome it all. These are very simple, yet effective, steps you can use to overcome your struggles.

Sometimes we just need those little clues or to hear from others who have walked in shoes similar to ours to feel reassured and empowered.

My mission and purpose is to walk hand-in-hand with you to a land of freedom, self-worth, self-love, and self-discovery.

DISCLAIMER

I understand it's much more convenient to play victim, but it only works for a short while. You gotta put skin in the game, quit the victim mindset of *why me*, and stop hosting pity parties if you truly want a life of abundance. The tools within this book will only work if you work with it! I refuse to believe in hand-me-downs (solely depending on someone else) or giving a man fish instead of teaching him how to fish, so he can fish for many more days – and when he pleases. I genuinely believe the more people learn to take charge of their lives, especially parents, and learn to fish vs. being given a fish, the happier and more responsible generations we will raise in our homes and society!

I urge you to not let this be another book on the shelf, a good read, or another thing taking up space in your purse. Let it be your manual for when you feel in doubt. Open yourself to receive and permit yourself to customize the steps in this book to fit your unique needs. I believe every person's journey and needs are different.

I do respect and recognize that not everyone is a believer and that even believers don't all believe in the same God. However, I am a woman of faith and throughout the book I will reference my Father in Heaven as Lord, Creator, God, and the Universe. I want you to know that this isn't a religious book in any shape or form. This book is authentically crafted to inspire all single mothers from all walks of life, backgrounds, colours, and shapes, and everyone else who reads it. Let's put our differences aside or better yet, see if we can toss them into the ocean. Let's fight for only one thing – the freedom to be ourselves no matter what!

As you will see through the book, I have not had the most desirable childhood, and my teen motherhood caused massive tension in our family, but I want to reassure you that we have mended and have an amazing bond! I will dig deeper and put heavy emphasis on the benefits of letting go and forgiving faster so you can start healing sooner, as well as not allowing yourself to be a victim of anyone's unaddressed problems. Together we will discover why this is an extremely important step for your happiness and health.

Through my stories, and those of the other powerful women who graciously shared their journeys and wisdom in this book, you will see that it is very possible to be a kick-ass mom in your own way, to be happy from inside out, to let go of the past that doesn't help you, and to live a life you desire on your own terms.

As a final note, please know that I am not a licensed doctor, therapist, or counsellor. The information within this book should not be construed as medical advice. Please check with your healthcare professional as needed.

1

Secret One

My Existence and Uniqueness Matter

I am glad you have stepped forward to reclaim your God-given power, and the right to live a purposeful and meaningful life.

Sistergirl, do you know the importance of your existence? Your uniqueness? Are you aware of the exceptional gifts you hold within you? Think about it for a moment. Do you know how crucial it is for you to remember and understand your worth and purpose? I will show you why it is crucial and how you can re-awaken your sense of self.

I know you have been hurt, betrayed, abused, mocked, and/or abandoned, but have you faced your past head-on and made peace with all that happened despite how awful it is? See, we can make peace with our past and work on healing so we can move on, or we can stay in a denial and a victim mindset by playing the blaming game. Until we confront our past head-on and allow ourselves to go within to heal, it is almost impossible to truly heal and move on. We can try to escape our past by turning to sex to feel loved and wanted, food for comfort, alcohol and drugs to forget our problems, workaholism to keep our minds busy, or gambling for entertainment, but none of these are authentic long-term solutions. They will do more harm than good. The real change and healing begin once you honestly confront your past, look at it dead straight in the eyes, speak to it, and let it go to make room for positive energy.

Honey, I know what it's like to feel rejected over and over, to be told you are lazy, stupid, and won't amount to anything in life. You begin to question why you exist and it feels like it's not for a good reason. You question your worth and if you even deserve to be here on Earth. You start to feel almost like an intruder existing under other people's shadows. I know what it's like to hold on to those unsolicited opinions that limit your beauty and potential.

Self-worth begins with an understanding of why you exist, trusting and believing in yourself, and recognizing that you are limitless. When you know your worth, you realize there is so much more to love about you.

If I could redo three things in my life, I would put more time in knowing my worth, loving myself more and sooner, and I'd take charge of my decisions!

At a very tender age, I suffered many losses. I didn't understand why it was happening. The amount of grief brought me to the point where I saw no use in living anymore.

Let me give you a little back story to help you understand when I first experienced and felt unworthy of love:

At around age four, a war erupted that cost me my daddy. My mom was a widow with four children and heavily pregnant. She ran to Uganda, a nearby country, to a refugee camp with all four of us. After a few months, refugees were about to be transferred to another camp far away. My grandmother had already been living in Uganda with one of my uncles; they had immigrated there when the first war broke out. Even though my mom had her mom and her elder brother in Uganda, they did not help her. Instead, their presence brought more chaos and anger.

My uncle told my mom he would build a house for her in Uganda on one of his lands, but she would have to take her sons back to her late husband's family first and only live with daughters. Boys are usually heirs, and I believe my uncle saw my brothers as liabilities to him if he let her stay there. My grandmother was very limited as she was also under my uncle's custody. When a husband dies, a son leads the family, and because my grandfather had died, my brother was the leader. My mother refused and decided she would rather sleep hungry and be with her children, and so she embarked on her refugee journey.

In African culture, it is normal and extremely important that grandparents have one of their grandchildren (often a girl) to help them around the house and keep them accompanied, especially if they are alone without a partner. Because I was the eldest girl of my siblings and was closer to my grandmother since birth, my grandmother requested my mom leave me behind with her as a companion and souvenir. From what I've heard, it wasn't an easy decision for my mom to make, but it was very important for her to know her mom had someone to talk with and to help her -- especially since mom didn't know where she was going or when she would see her mother again. My mom was the last born of five children, so their bond was very strong.

My mom made this choice out of kindness and for the love of her mom, but it cost me so much and caused me to hate her immensely.

Now, we were not extraordinarily rich growing up, but we were far from being poor. My uncle was a very respected pastor, a builder, a businessman, and a farmer. His two eldest sons both had businesses and other things going. My grandmother was a farmer and a businesswoman as well, and from what I hear, before my father died, we did not lack food, nice clothing, or a roof.

With my uncle and grandmother, I now lived in a large compound that had three houses, which was fenced by a large, tall stone fence with a gate. In our compound there was one big bungalow that had many bedrooms in it, with two front doors and two back doors. In addition to the bungalow, there were two other houses. One of them belonged to my uncle's second son (the first one lived elsewhere) and the other belonged to my three other cousins who had lost both their parents early in life. These cousins were also under my uncle's custody, and maybe all the responsibility was why he was so miserable.

This large fence was surrounded by very fruitful, large avocado trees, lots of banana trees with bananas hanging, and a lot of yams and other vegetables in the mix.

My grandmother and I had lived on the left side of the bungalow, and my uncle with his wife and children lived on the right side of the bungalow. There were two totally different homes in that bungalow. Grandma and I had our own entrance, our own kitchen, and did our own thing.

Grandma and I lived relatively undisturbed and blissful for quite some time.

When I was around ten years old, the unthinkable happened. My grandmother, the only mother I had, my shield and protector, the woman I had grown to fall in love with -- died suddenly. At this point, it had been about six years since I had last seen my mom or my siblings. My mom wasn't able to come to my grandmother's funeral because there was no way to communicate. My mom learned of her mother's death long after they had buried her through someone who knew my family and was visiting the refugee camp my mom was in. At around that same time, my mom just had another baby, who I would meet three years later.

After my grandmother's death, I felt so much emptiness. I felt lost. I was scared because I had observed my uncle treating my three orphaned cousins like rotten trash. I felt as though I was sinking somewhere in the ocean all by myself with no one to call out to for help. It was like being dropped somewhere in a desert from a helicopter. I thought things couldn't get any worse, but I hadn't seen anything yet.

My long suffering of emotional, physical, and sexual abuse began immediately after the funeral.

Her death robbed me of so much, including my childhood and innocence. It brought me so much anger. I felt abandoned and hopeless. While still mourning my grandmother, I was accused of theft by my own uncle. The same man who would take over my guardianship believed that my grandmother (his mother) had lots of money and, because I was the only one living with her and based on the way she adored me, he believed she must have left the money with me. He and his two sons beat me up (kicked, slapped, pinched my ears, used rods, or anything they could get a hold of) hoping I would open my mouth and tell them where the money was. They were convinced that I had the knowledge of where my grandmother kept her money and that I had access to it.

They would lift me up by my ears, and my uncle would kick me with his work boots. He would also instruct his wife to not give me food and instructed many other forms of torture. The truth to this day is that I knew Grandma had money, but I had no clue where she kept it. There was not even one coin left with me by my grandmother. In fact, I didn't know my grandmother was sick until I woke up in the middle of the night and found many people sitting in our compound with a big fire going. I heard lots of noise and crying, and when I asked what was wrong, I was told my grandmother had died. (I will never forget this day.) Now I was left without a mom or a dad and my grandmother, who had been my rock, had left me.

Shortly thereafter, my uncle started gaslighting and shaming me by saying that my mother had left me, and now he must take on the responsibility of feeding and clothing me. He went on to say that he would take me back to my father's family, who I didn't even know. I didn't know my mom and sibling's whereabouts. I felt rejected and unwanted. It felt like I was being passed on from hand-to-hand like a tennis ball to people who didn't even want me. Uncle didn't know how to whisper or use an inside voice. He didn't have a filter for his mouth and would say what he wanted, when he wanted -- no matter who was around.

For an exceptionally long time, I felt such a big void from never experiencing a father's love, especially when my uncle would shower his daughter with so much love and so many gifts. This feeling stuck with me for many years until I learned how to deal with it by redirecting my thoughts. I would be lying if I said the void feeling doesn't occasionally sneak up on me even to this day, particularly when I am going through a crisis. I craved for father's love so much to the point I would seek love from older men, who often took advantage of me, hoping they would treat me how a father would treat his daughter.

I wasn't so much interested in relationships between a man and a woman, as I just wanted to feel how a little girl would feel in her father's loving arms. This void and mindset caused me to over-give myself in many dishonouring relationships in hopes of having a happy family. I wanted to make sure my children would never have to feel the same void as I did, but that dream was out of reach.

This void became very real and manifested itself when my grandmother died; perhaps it was because my grandmother loved me to pieces and made sure I was entertained and comfortable in every way possible. My auntie, who lived nearby, repeatedly requested my uncle release me into her care, but he refused. To this day, I don't understand why not since I was such a burden to him.

I remember a day that repeatedly played itself in my head for years: I was working in the garden one extremely hot summer day. A remarkably close family friend showed up where I was working and greeted me, as usual. He picked a few weeds in the garden near where I was working and then made his way to what I thought would be his exit. He stood behind a tree and called to me saying he wanted to show me something. As I approached him and bent to see what he was trying to "show" me, he knocked me on the ground, forcefully lifted my skirt, aggressively pulled down my underwear, and combatively forced his nakedness into mine.

I had just turned eleven years old, barely had any breast, and this would be the first time I would experience vaginal bleeding. I remember trying to scream and him slapping my mouth, pressing down on it, and squeezing my jaws. I can still hear his voice threatening that if I dared to say anything or scream, he would make up lies and tell my uncle about it. I can also remember how I could barely walk, as I was in agony, and had to hide at the back of the fence behind an avocado tree. There I stayed for hours, crying and shaking uncontrollably, while wondering what I would tell my uncle or auntie (his wife) if they were to see me walking like that.

That night, I was in an immeasurable amount of pain and could not sleep. I had millions of questions running through my mind and memories one after another. But I was so terrified of my uncle that I couldn't open my mouth to tell them what happened and what I had seen, which was replaying in my mind. The feeling is awful for anyone, but even worse for an eleven-year-old who couldn't understand what happened to her, why it happened, and what was going on with her body. Unfortunately, his first act would not be the last. I hated my life and everyone else around me; I felt they had all contributed to my pain.

The day after this incident, my family thought I had gone mad. I remember them gathering around me in the middle of our compound, ensuring the gate door was closed while questioning me about what I was seeing and if I was okay.

According to the family members around me, out of nowhere I started jumping, running, screaming, and pointing at things shouting, "The snake! The man!" and fought every one of them who tried to hold me down.

I had gotten overwhelmed and couldn't contain myself anymore. While the act of the man who violated me was going on, I had seen what looked like a snake as I tried to turn my head fighting. I could almost see it come to sting me while not having a way to get up and run, speak, or turn my head fully to see.

I became bitter and suspicious of everybody around me. I hated my mom for not coming to my rescue sooner, despite all the calls from her sister (she had received the letter and now there was a phone communication) about the abuse I was being put through by her brother. I became fearful about everything I did because even simple things like using my left hand (I was left-handed) and laughing about things I found funny were irritating and unacceptable to my uncle. (My grandmother was hilarious and so, by default, I laughed very often.) I grew resentful and jealous of my cousins (uncle's children) and quickly learned that I was in this game of life alone for the long haul.

My uncle would torture us by beating us, calling us all kinds of mean words, and by not giving us food; however, he ensured his children and I went to school and had uniforms. This wasn't the case for my orphaned cousins, though. They didn't have food or clothing on top of the never-ending insults.

After many months of this man's abuse, I developed a "I hate everyone including myself and I don't care" attitude. I started sneaking out occasionally when an opportunity presented itself and offered my body for food or whatever else I needed. I had to learn to sell my body for food and undergarments at age eleven, but unfortunately, it was not just me.

Sadly, one of my three orphaned cousins started selling her body so she and her siblings could get food. She also started stealing and unfortunately, to this day, still struggles with these practices she did out of need. They have now become habits. No matter how much money you give her, nor what amazing husband she gets or the beautiful children she has, now and then she will just pack up and leave everything behind without cause or to go steal -- not because she is hungry or in need of clothing. It's a real struggle for her. On the bright side, the other two cousins are amazing parents and are happily married!

One fateful day, after about three years of sufferings inflicted by my uncle, his two sons, and the man who continuously sexually abused me, my auntie Esther came to visit as usual. It was a celebration day for me whenever she came to visit because I knew I would eat, play with the other children, and there would be no unjustifiable beatings that looked like killing a snake.

She came and saw the pain in my eyes, saw how my body was changing rapidly, and asked me how I was doing. All I could do was burst into tears and fall into her arms. She hugged me very tightly and during this hug, the only thing that was going through my mind was, *Please take me with you.* My heart raced with itself saying, *Tell her what that guy (abuser) is doing to you.* But I knew it wouldn't go well because she would confront my uncle, and if my uncle refused to let me go with her, then I would pay for it heavily after she left. Lord behold; after my auntie had done her own observations and left, she realized I was in grave danger but was both limited and helpless as to how to save me.

Shortly after this visit, someone she knew was traveling to the camp where it was said my mom and siblings were, and my auntie sent a message with her for my mom: "Your mom has died and been buried, but your child may be next. It would be in your best interest to make a choice to come pick up your child while she is still breathing, or you may have to come pick up her casket."

Thankfully, my mom heard my auntie's plea, and she came to pick me up! According to mom, she couldn't sleep after getting this message and had to do everything within her power to get transportation for her and her son (a new brother I would meet for the first time), as well as mine. I was relieved, and I was excited to finally meet my siblings, who I could not even remember. In fact, when my mom came, I could not remember her, either. It was basically like meeting strangers that you have a blood connection with and you have to build a relationship from scratch. We were re-introduced as mom and daughter and siblings. This was a honeymoon that would end shortly after.

Soon, the reality kicked in. I was now the elder girl in the house, and in African culture, that meant I was expected to do almost all the cooking and cleaning. On top of that, my mom was a midwife. So, she was gone for most nights or would be called in the middle of the night. She was a farmer up and off to the farm by 5:00 a.m. and a businesswoman gone for most afternoons.

At around 2:00 p.m., farming would be over if she planned to go to the market or had other important meetings. If so, she wouldn't be back home until everyone was in bed (between 11:00 p.m. and 1:00 a.m.), which meant I was the mother of the house to ensure everyone was taken care of and fed, and the home and our very large compound was clean, in addition to school and gardening. My mom was also a host at heart, so we had never-ending guests, especially on

Sabbath day (Saturday); we would have to cook up a storm.

During this time, I also had to learn a new way of living because, as much as we had both been living in Uganda, we were speaking different languages and had been living different cultures. It was literally a completely different way of doing things. I had been living in the Kisoro district and adopted to a Baganda/ Bafumbira lifestyle, while my family was living in a Kyangwali refugee settlement (a home to more than 83,000 refugees formed by a majority of Congolese, which meant they spoke and did things the Congolese way).

A good example of this was when I was in Kisoro. Kiswahili was seen as a bandit or army language because it was mostly used by soldiers who didn't really have a good reputation (known for having multiple women and corruption). And here I was. This Swahili, as well as Runyoro (the camp was in Bunyoro land), was going to be one of my new languages in order to thrive in the camp. Another great example of difference was food. Growing up in Kisoro, we had cassava trees as flowers and in this refugee camp, it was one of the most eaten and cherished vegetables.

I had to learn these things, and much more, in order to fit into my new community. Everyone tried to make me feel welcome, but for a long time, I felt like an outsider because my siblings would laugh and make fun of me whenever I said something in Kifumbila. I was the only one who spoke differently, behaved differently, didn't have the sibling bond like my other five siblings, and I didn't even like most of the food (I wasn't used to them).

Africa is big and it may seem like most people do things the same, but even in just one country there are multiple cultures that do not come easily for even a born-and-raised African.

Soon enough, my siblings nicknamed me "lazy" and said grandma spoiled me. They started comparing me to my little sister who was a badass worker, and this really got to me. My mom tried so hard to make up for missed years whenever she could. (I think she felt guilty about leaving me behind and what I endured after my grandmother's death, even though it wasn't her fault.) Soon enough, I was labelled "mom's favourite" when, in actuality, I was not feeling it nor seeing it. (I was mad and got caught up into a space that eventually led to entitlement and ignorance of mom's efforts.) I was still mad at her for leaving me behind, abandoning me (I felt), and for not coming to my rescue sooner. My siblings also started body shaming me by comparing my head to that of a monkey because my hair came up to my forehead and resembled that of a monkey. As we grew up, they said this was a joke, but personally, I hadn't taken it rightly and was always self-conscious about it.

As time went by, our eldest brother visibly became harsh toward me, which woke the monster in me. My healing scars became wounds again. He believed I was lazy, and mom was too easy on me. He constantly called me lazy, foolish, stupid, and a complainer, whenever I would ask my little sisters to do something. I started missing many days of school to go work on the farm, and he started beating me much more than the others because, apparently, as an elder girl I should know this and that. I guess I didn't check off all his expectations of an elder girl.

To make matters worse, because he was older and because mom was a widow, he was next of kin and the one mom would go to for advice. His say was a big deciding factor in our family decisions and almost whatever he said was what went. I refuse to believe my brother was or is a bad person; he had experienced so many traumas, like war unfolding before his eyes, our uncle not wanting him and my brother, coming from a comfortable life to a refugee life, and being forced to grow up so fast in order to be the man of the house at a very young age. It didn't give him time to process things or deal with them properly. He internalized a lot of things in an effort to "be a man" and didn't fully take the time to face them head-on or seek help.

I was slowly settling into my new normal, and as much as it was hard, it was nothing compared to what I had gone through with my uncle.

About a year later, my mom's good friend became ill (may she continue to rest in peace) and my mom decided I was the best person to send away again. As per mom, they specifically requested for me and, as hard as it was hard for her, she couldn't see herself denying someone help when they needed it most. She said yes to them and sent me to be a helper, which really meant I was a maid/nanny.

Again, I became very confused and terribly angry, but children were taught not to question their parents or elders. So, I obeyed and did as instructed. The main reason I felt so confused by this move was because her friend had a mom, three sisters, and brothers who could have helped her. Why send me? She had a sister who was my friend and was around my age, and she had an unmarried sister who was much older than me. She also had a sister who was a little younger than me who could have done those basic chores like cooking, entertaining her niece, and cleaning.

I could not ask my mom these questions as I would look like, or sound as if, I was being disrespectful. For that, I possibly would have gotten beaten up. I packed and went. Although the treatment wasn't bad at my mom's best friend's home, I did not get to go to school once during the months I spent there "helping" (while her husband knew the importance of education). At that time, this made me even more angry because I felt unwanted. I missed my grandmother who wanted me, loved me, and nurtured me. The woman who put my needs before hers. A mother who sat me down when the dark fell to tell me stories by the fire. I missed my best friend. We would visit her friends together to have local alcohol (homemade and children friendly).

I found no meaning to life and wondered if it would be better to just end my life and go meet her wherever she was. I asked myself many questions: *What mother, who has not seen her child for many years, just sends her away again instead of focusing on building a strong relationship -- when there are many other options? What if I was not here? Who was she going to send? Why would this woman's husband claim to be a Christian attending Christian university, even though he is already educated, can't think of educating me as well? Is she really my mother or did they lie to me and a wrong woman picked me up? Am I really just here to help or did her friend pay her? Why didn't she send my younger sisters? What is going on in my sibling's minds? Why isn't my eldest brother talking to her about this? Why didn't she let her bestie ask one of her sisters? What were the arrangements between them? Why isn't mom's bestie thinking of putting me in school rather than washing clothes, cooking, cleaning, and entertaining their daughter?*

These questions, and many more, ran through my mind and were never answered until my book was almost complete. (Look out for the second book in this series where I explain how we finally sat down as a family and had a healing conversation.)

Finally, the time came and they sent me back home. I needed to reconnect and pick up where I left off. It was not easy as I now had a new set of questions in my mind. Now, there was this constant feeling of *I do not belong.* More questions emerged, along with negative thoughts, such as, *Why am I here anyway? I am not good enough; I am lazy and useless. I wonder why nobody wants me. It looks like even my own mother doesn't want me.*

Shortly after getting back home, another good friend of my mom's was moving, and my mom decided to buy his house, which was in a better location and much nicer than the one we had.

In that neighbourhood there was a gentleman who coincidentally was named Isaac, which would be Rebecca's husband in the Bible! Girl: This man was an angel sent my way in a human form!

He seemed much older than I was, went to the same church we went to, and soon enough, he won my mother and brother's heart with his kindness. He even became my safe haven. He wasn't educated, but he was better off financially than most people from farming. He would hire people to work for him and would have trucks come to buy the crops at his home. He farmed everything from corn, beans, potatoes, sugar cane, yams, etc.

Isaac became my negotiator and advocated for me -- even offering to pay someone to work in my place so I could go to school. I would go to "work" for him in order to buy myself undergarments and other feminine items I needed. I wasn't comfortable asking my mom for all my needs since my uncle made us show him our undergarments to prove we needed more. Isaac tried many things to lessen my workload, such as offering to cook a little on some Fridays. Whenever we had a church youth meeting far from home, he would always make sure my meals were taken care of while there, and he would reserve my seat on his bike (transportation). Speaking of a bike, Issac was the one who taught me how to ride a bicycle.

The list of his goodness is far too long to list, but one thing stood out to me the most. Once, through our conversation, he discovered I was sleeping many nights outside. I would fall asleep during a dinner conversation because we mostly ate outside when the weather was good, and I was a deep sleeper. It wasn't a walk in the park to wake me up. You had to shake me aggressively or pour water on me to wake me up. So, my family gave up trying to wake me, and I would spend the night outside on the floor or sleep there until I woke up in the middle of the night and then went to bed.

Every night before Issac would go to bed, he would come over and make sure I wasn't outside. He would even knock on my window to ensure I was in bed (my bed was by the window).

For these reasons and more, he became my confidant. One day, I was fed-up with all the bitterness I was carrying (and the feeling of not fitting into my own family or even wanted by anyone). A thought flashed through my mind like a heavy wind, *Why continue bothering? What is the point of living anyway?*

I remembered that someone had said that if you swallow a battery or eat the insides, you can die because it was poison. I quickly told my brother I was going to the garden to get something to cook and went to ask Isaac for money. I told him I needed to buy something. I got the money and waited until my brother went for his soccer practice so I could go buy my batteries.

Later that evening, after buying the batteries, I began working on the flowers behind our house while waiting for darkness to fall so I could execute my plan, when Isaac came out of nowhere just to have a conversation. Because of all his kindness and devotion to me, I decided that if anyone needed to know, it would be him. He meant the world to me. I opened up and told him of my plans. I told him I couldn't push on any longer, and I just wanted to thank him for everything (he was aware of my feelings and struggles all along as he was the person I vented to regularly). He begged, cried, and said I would never understand how much joy I brought to his life, and he promised to do everything within his power to see me happy and comfortable. He didn't leave that evening and stayed until we all went to bed. He was back to check on me first thing in the morning.

Isaac didn't have any family in the refugee camp, nor anyone nearby. In order for him to get to his family, he would have to take a bus for at least two days. I saw the pain in his eyes, which was the same pain I had gone through. I knew that pain, which is why I decided to keep my life, and I'm so grateful I did. The pain in his eyes was too much for me to bear, and I promised I would not go ahead with the suicide plan. He kept constantly checking on me, kept speaking life into me, asking if I needed anything, and soon enough the feeling no longer haunted me.

My friendship with Isaac grew even closer until one day when a young, handsome photographer named Joe started expressing interest in me becoming his girlfriend. This young man started sending me cute love letters through a mutual friend (our school Head Boy at the time) and would slip a few coins in with his love letters. He started dropping in at my school, coming to our church, which was a roughly forty-five minutes to one-hour walk from his home. I felt quite excited because -- finally! Someone other than Isaac found me attractive and wanted me! It's fair to note that he was also quite a charm in his letters and was educated, which was one of the credentials I had for my future husband.

With all the excitement, I figured there was no better person to share the good news with other than Isaac and one of my other girlfriends (my mom's bestie's little sister that I went to help/nanny).

This girlfriend of mine eventually betrayed me by telling one of my cousins about this man, along with everything she knew about him. She also gave my cousin the pictures of us that I had entrusted in her care because I didn't want my family to see them nor know about this newfound love.

My family eventually burned the pictures before my eyes, and the beatings I got were so bad that I wasn't able to walk properly for about three days.

From that day forward, the beatings became my daily bread each time they saw him around me, or saw him pass by, and they closely supervised me each time he came around because they knew he was looking for me. Why they hated him so much is best known to them, but I strongly believe it was because he was from a different country and was new to the camp (this kind of mixture was rare in those days, unlike today).

While it was hard, I am thankful there are people who can keep secrets. Our Head Boy that Joe sent the letters through never told anyone, and I am grateful for that.

Sistergirl, after sharing the news with Isaac, what shocked me the most was his response. It was far from what I expected. He responded by expressing how much he loved me (romantically). I knew I could not handle losing Isaac, but he wasn't checking off the boxes of my fantasy future husband. He wasn't educated, not dark, nor tall; I knew he was kind, but I didn't know if he was romantic since he hadn't made a move. I found every fault as to why he wasn't the one, and the list grew longer and longer (you know how we ladies design our future husbands). Weeks went by and Joe kept on his game while Isaac also kept on with his. After giving it a long thought, and feeling as confused as hell, I knew I had to make a choice as I was playing with fire.

My choice came from a place of need and guilt. I felt like there was no other way I could repay Isaac for what he had done for me other than giving him the only thing I had -- my heart -- and eventually, my body, which led to getting pregnant not too long after that at the age of sixteen.

I couldn't master the courage to tell Joe of my decision, so I avoided him at all cost until we got to Canada and my family restricted me from using the phone.

My mom had been working on getting our family to Canada for a very long time, and a few months after I got pregnant, she got word that our visa was out (approved visa to travel to Canada). She decided to move us to Hoima (a town a few hours away outside of camp), but when we moved, I didn't know I was pregnant yet, although I was feeling a bit funny. I didn't know who to ask. Isaac and I had jokingly talked about having a baby, not knowing that I was about two weeks pregnant.

A few days after we moved, I started feeling strange and was exhausted. I started feeling sleepier and noticed a black line on my tummy. Near where we lived was a lady who had gone to school with us in the refugee camp. She had been impregnated by the son of one of my mom's good friends. She was later abandoned by the biological father. I confided in this lady, asked her how to find out if you are pregnant, and sure enough, she confirmed I was pregnant. She offered to give me medication or to take me where people could help me abort the baby. I told her I didn't want to die because I heard that many schoolgirls were dying while aborting. I promised her the world if she didn't tell anyone. We tried using her phone to call Isaac to no avail and I went back home. My mom and two elder brothers had gone back to the refugee camp to take care of harvesting crops and selling things while my younger siblings and I waited in town.

About a week after this lady confirmed I was pregnant, my second brother came to bring us more food. When he was about to leave, I crafted up a letter addressed to Isaac informing him of the situation. Girl, this was life and death, and honestly, I didn't think he was going to give it to him or leave it unopened, but I knew this was my only choice at this point.

To my surprise, less than three days later, Isaac came fully equipped to support me in every way possible and stayed until it was our time to board the plane to Canada (roughly about three months).

Now, I don't know what my family was thinking while he was staying with us (my younger siblings and I) while both my elder brothers and mom were in the refugee camp. But this man took complete care of me till the last day, and I will be forever thankful to him. If I craved for an avocado, fried cassava or bananas (those were the things I craved the most), he would go to every market possible or stand by the street until he got whatever I wanted. He would not let me wash clothes or cook; he would do it or bribe my little sisters to do it for me. He became my pillow whenever I needed to nap. Actually, one of my mom's good friend stopped by while I was resting my head on his lap, and I was afraid he would tell my mom, but thank goodness he never did!

Then, a dark day came when I was five months pregnant. It was time to take a trip of what would be my family's dream come true. Since I was under eighteen and we were not married, I had to make peace with leaving the father of my child behind in Africa to migrate to Canada. We looked at every possible situation: from escaping to a different country or city, to telling Immigration so we could stay together, but none of it looked possible. Our best option was to escape to another town far away, but we both knew that if the entire family missed a lifetime opportunity because of us, then we would never forgive ourselves. We decided to have a Plan A and B in place, which was to go with the flow and hopefully all would go well. If things didn't go well and Immigration said my family couldn't go, then we would escape to a nearby town. At the time, Immigration made it difficult to travel while pregnant, especially after your fifth month, and they often made you wait until you gave birth first and then resume the process. It all depended on the doctor who worked on your file, and we were afraid it would devastate my family to wait longer.

I had hidden my romantic relationship and pregnancy from my family. Now it was time for the news to be revealed to them by an Immigration medical doctor that I was five months pregnant. My mom was a midwife and could have easily figured it out, but she couldn't since she stayed in the camp while my younger siblings and I were in town.

They were furious after finding out. I remember, on our way back to the hotel (Immigration rented a hotel for us for three days before our travel) how my eldest brother kept looking at me and made a statement I will never forget: "I don't play around and if you are not careful, I will push you onto the road and let the vehicles kill you because people like you are only here to cause problems and shame."

Based on how I knew him, I did not doubt nor second guess it. From that point on, I started avoiding him at all costs and walking as far from him as I could while keeping calm. I immediately shifted and went as far from the road as I could. I also saw fear in my mother's eyes, though she said nothing about my brother's comment. Through the night and the next two days, she made sure I was as far away as possible from him -- especially after he made his second comment referring to my pregnancy: "If you are not careful, I will beat you until that bastard comes out."

Sistergirl, I love Canada, and I am a very proud African Canadian, but my journey to Canada isn't very rosy or as exciting as many.

The boarding day came (a dream come true for my mom and siblings) and I only had one wish. We had been in a hotel for three days, and all I wanted was to see Isaac so I could say goodbye and hug him one last time. That didn't happen. He was among many people who would accompany us to the airport (At this point the family still didn't know he was the father to be. Only Isaac, myself, and the lady knew), but the vehicle he was in got delayed and found us already gone. I travelled feeling sad, angry, and wondering why we didn't just go with our Plan B and escape. But I knew what coming to Canada meant for my family and didn't want them to miss the opportunity of a lifetime because of me. This would be the last time I see Isaac face-to-face (it has been fourteen years now).

2

Secret Two
Broken and Lost, but Hopeful

I worried about how I would raise my baby as a single mom with no support in a foreign country, but I had hope. I hoped that I could do something to ensure Isaac joined me so we could continue our little family we had started.

I understood that this wasn't the end of the journey, but the beginning. I understood clearly that I would need to be strong for myself, but more importantly for my baby on the way. I told myself on a daily basis that giving up was no longer an option, as now I had a beautiful gift to live for.

After arriving in Canada, I told my family who the father was and they restricted me from speaking to him. (The reason I kept the father of my child a secret from my family in Africa was because I feared he would have been thrown in jail since I was considered a minor, my mom had influence, and the family was very angry.) Soon after our arrival, I was restricted from many things, including communicating with him or using the phone at all without permission.

Whenever Joe, Jim (our Head Boy who was the messenger between me and Joe), or Isaac called, they would hang up the phone on them, and eventually both Joe and Isaac got tired and moved on with their lives.

After arriving in Canada, I went to school briefly before my mom and the so-called workers Immigration had sent to support us decided that "pregnant women don't go to school."

When I complained and tried to fight their decision, I remember my mom asking me, "So if you knew you wanted to go to school, why did you open your legs?"

I became the cook and the cleaner. Physical and emotional abuse became my daily dose. I became the one to pick and drop off our youngest brother to and from school. The cravings of a pregnant woman meant nothing to my mother, who knew it well enough after having seven children (one died as a baby) and after working with pregnant women for so long as a midwife. The so-called workers the Immigration had assigned to help us turned their ears away. They were supposed to report the abuse, but they encouraged it instead. The sad part was that one of the workers was a pastor, or some church elder, and the other was a mom herself.

I didn't know what it was like to sit in the living room with everyone and watch TV or enjoy each other's company without being mocked or verbally abused, so I decided to keep to myself in my bedroom, which I shared with my two younger sisters.

After living in Canada for two months, I joined a program called Healthy

Babies Healthy Children (HBHC)[1], which is a free home-visiting program that supports moms to have a healthy pregnancy, develop a positive relationship with their child, promotes your child's growth and development, and connects you to resources and programs within your community.

Because my English was very limited, they sent me a translator who spoke Swahili. She came during the day when I was the only one at home, so we could have open conversation. She asked me many questions, did her own observations, and immediately got me help. She called a shelter for abused women who then sent me a taxi immediately. I grabbed a few of my belongings, and off I went to become free from abuse (at about seven months pregnant).

After arriving at the shelter, I blocked the shelter number and called my eldest brother to tell him where I had left the keys for when they got home. I also informed him that I would not be able to pick up or drop off my little brother moving forward, so they would have to make arrangements among themselves. He was shocked because I didn't go anywhere on my own other than picking up my brother or going to the store when they sent me to buy things for them.

While on the phone with him, he asked, "Where are you?"

I told him, "I don't know."

"When are you coming home?"

"I don't know."

This would be the last time I spoke or saw my family for months. I wouldn't see them again until after my baby was born (seven months pregnant to two weeks post-partum).

After leaving home, I reconnected with Isaac over the phone, but sadly, he had lost hope and started entangling with another woman, which brought our relationship to an end.

I had kept in touch with a few ladies from a Baptist church, and they would visit me occasionally. These ladies came to see the baby and eventually convinced me to go show my family by saying my mom missed me. I gave them a hard time, but eventually listened. Sure enough, we were all missing each other!

Sistergirl, I wouldn't say my family and I have a perfect relationship because no family does, but I must say we have an unbelievably beautiful relationship given where we have been -- and I am forever grateful for it! We all worked hard to move past all the traumas we had experienced during this time in our different ways and for our different reasons. I also speak to Isaac on a biweekly, some-

---

1 See references for details.

times weekly basis, and he has moved to America to experience "the American dream" with his wife and children.

I am sure by now you can see that I know a thing or two about disappointment, resentment, feeling unworthy, feeling unloved, and what it's like to feel like there's no drive or purpose to live for. No matter what you are going through, you can choose to be your greatest cheerleader or greatest critic.

Now think of what I went through emotionally after finding out that Isaac had moved on. *He couldn't wait a little longer to fight for our family as much as I wanted to? Another rejection? I guess he was just using me and maybe didn't love me. I hate him.* I experienced so many negative thoughts that could have easily taken me down the hill, but with a baby this time.

At the time, I didn't know what it was called and why it was important, but I started doing affirmations. I started looking at my precious baby, who I named Hope, as my "why" – my reason to hang on another day and then another day. I started speaking life into myself and intentionally found something to help me push on, which was my baby, food, a roof, and a life in general, as that's basically all I had. I would be naïve if I didn't thank the amazing ladies (staff) at St. Monica's house (a shelter for young moms), particularly the two (J & E) who had helped me through the after my baby was born. I also thank my sister friend Lissy Rosey, Heather (staff) at the pregnancy resource centre, Ruth, Elsa, and many other amazing people who became my rock during this time.

As years went by, I realized it's not fair or even logical to expect others to see my value if, personally, I was too blind to see it myself. To ask others to see and embrace all the amazing things within me, while I, as the source and the ultimate carrier didn't see it, was irrational. I came to realize that I could outsource many things and services, but happiness cannot be outsourced. You can't send someone to buy it for you regardless of the cash in your account.

Honey, I do not care if you were conceived by accident; you are not on Earth by accident. Your mother could have aborted you, taken Plan B, or taken her life the moment she found out she was pregnant; the fact that she carried you for however many months, gave birth to you, nurtured you (or another mama nurtured you), and you are here reading this book, it was not by accident, my friend. If you think or feel you do not belong or feel unwanted like I did, then I want to remind you that you are meant to be here today 110 percent, and you are very much needed!

Sistergirl, pause for a moment and look at all the successful people you admire like actresses, TV hosts, musicians, and motivational speakers. Think of one thing they have in common. Not all, but most of them, had their breakthrough come after disappointments and discouragements. Think of Steve Harvey, Oprah, Lisa Nichols, and many more.

Recognize the gifts and opportunities that come during turmoil and commit to never defining yourself by the circumstances you went through, or are going through, nor by what anyone believes you can't be or do. You are so much more and bigger than those circumstances or words. You are worthy, you were created for a purpose, you are gorgeous, and yes you, my friend, are a damn powerhouse!

People will always have unsolicited opinions about what you are and disappointments will always come, but when you are aware of yourself, your purpose, your worth, and the great value you bring to the world, you are unshakable!

Sistergirl, think of who you could be raising in your home today. Your child could be a doctor saving lives, a pastor bringing many lives to Christ, a teacher, a president leading a nation, a lawyer fighting for justice, inspirational speaker motivating the masses and speaking life into others, a loving stay-at-home mom to our future generations -- anything they decide to do. Can you imagine the impact and the value you are adding to the world alone just by doing your due diligence raising your child/children?

Now, think of it: If you could step out boldly and powerfully and listen to your heart calling – what do you think would happen? Then think of the value you bring into this world – it's massive! Do not get discouraged or throw in the towel on your desires because of the lies others installed into you. You are not here coincidently; you are God's crafted masterpiece, ordained to be here for a purpose.

There are 7.8 billion people in the world, but you, my friend, are unique and there can be only one you! Think about it. I think that's epic! It is very impressive that we can buy the same house as our neighbours, same outfits, same cars, travel to the same destinations, do the same careers or businesses as them, and even do a lot of plastic surgeries to look like them, but the truth remains that we are unique and special in our own ways. Honey, you are original and IMPOSSIBLE to duplicate! So, if this is the case, then why not embrace and acknowledge how special you are?

I know there will always be negative voices and sometimes they can be so loud they overshadow the positive ones. It can make it hard to get up one day and proclaim, "I will embrace and love my life the way it is." Negative thoughts will always make their way into your ears, but there is a saying that says: A thankful heart is a happy heart. I could not agree more.

Any negative feelings you hold about yourself did not develop overnight; it was a consistent flow of incidents that built until you believed them and began walking in them. It will require the same effort for you to break them. Think, speak, and act intentionally as you break this cycle and start meditating on gratitude and affirmations. In fact, you may have to work triple to break those curses. Here is what the greatest book ever written said about the power of our words:

"The tongue has the power of life and death, and those who love it will eat its fruit" (Proverbs 18:21).

What fruits are you planting with the power of your tongue? What we think and say about ourselves is so powerful that, until we change our language and how we think or talk to ourselves, it's nearly impossible to step out into our greatness. For those who are religious or Bible readers, God did not take clay or anything to create anybody or anything; the Bible says he created the world using his words.

"In the beginning was the Word, and the Word was with God, and the Word was God" (John 1:1).

"And God said, "Let there be light" and there was light" (Genesis 1:3).

While writing this book, I faced a lot of discouragement and disappointments, but during one of my coaching sessions, my coach looked into my eyes and said, "Rebecca, there is so much gold in the turmoil, there are lots of opportunities during this COVID19, but you have to keep your head high." That is absolutely true! You will go through many disappointments, discouragement and yes, you may feel upset along the way, but never give up. There is always a light at the end of the tunnel, but only if you keep going will you see the light at the end. Don't define yourself by your struggles as they are only here temporarily to teach you something and pave a way for your next breakthrough -- and off it's gone!

One of my greatest and most profound tools for overcoming discouragement has been gratitude. Gratitude is often overlooked, but it can work wonders in your life if you practice it regularly. Science has repeatedly proven that the benefits of practicing gratitude are endless[2].

By taking time to acknowledge and reflect on the amazing people, things, and your abundance in life, you give yourself a reason to push on for another day. You then experience positive emotions and develop compassion for others, who may not quite be as fortunate as you are. Gratitude strengthens the relationship with yourself and others. Gratitude allows you to shift your focus to the beautiful opportunities waiting for you on the other side instead of being rooted into whatever you are going through.

Commit to finding ten beautiful things for every ugly thing you see and tell yourself that giving up is not an option. After all, whatever has a beginning has an end. This is just a phase, and this too shall come to pass.

If you are ever going to practice one thing in your life, let it be gratitude. I put heavy importance on gratitude because I believe that if you can't be thankful for the small things in your life, then it will be nearly impossible to be thankful for bigger things. Why? Because the chances are you will be too busy looking for bigger things and won't notice when they arrive. Taking the time to be grateful for what you have and the amazing people in your life is an art that soothes your mind and soul. Many people make the mistake of focusing on what is not going well, rather than focusing and putting energy on those beautiful things they do have going well.

You do not need to have much, nor have everything figured out, in order to do this practice. All you need is to use one of your five senses to see, smell, touch, taste, or hear and some quiet time.

Oftentimes, when I find myself complaining about what I don't have and falling into a wishy-washy kind of mode, I quickly take some time to embrace who I am and what I have. For example, I would be so thankful for having three healthy bouncing babies who light up my world and even would take the time to say a prayer for those who could not have children, not by choice. I would be so thankful for my dearest family and friends who still pick me up and show me love even after they didn't agree with my decisions (that ultimately led to my brokenness). I would be thankful for a roof over my head, even if it may not be my ideal home. I would be so thankful for my job that put food on the table for

---

2   See reference page for details.

my children, even if it may not be my dream job. I would be so thankful for my tenacity and resilience to continue pushing on despite my long list of financial loses, relationship losses, and so much abuse endured at a young age. I would be thankful for silly things like my car that makes it from work to home.

When you develop a positive, thankful attitude, you become less entitled to what people, the government, and everybody else "should" be doing for you, and you become a problem-solver! You are less bothered by haters or those who I call vibe and happiness killers.

Sistergirl, I know you may be thinking, *Where the heck do I get time?* or *But, Rebecca, I don't have anything to be thankful for.* Oh yes, you do. Take a good look around and take a deeper look again. Turn on your television or get on your phone and look at the floods, shootings, hungry children, or visit a children's hospital. Look around when you are driving in winter, and look at those moms pushing strollers in that snow or in the rain. Even better, go spend one hour at the soup kitchen in your community for the next five days, and I am sure by the end you will have a million things to be thankful for. Think of how many people commit suicide daily because they forgot to realize how blessed they are. Do not stress about the how; just concentrate on finding whatever is good in your life and focus your energy on that. You will be amazed at how wonderful you feel.

Time? You do not need a lot of time for this quick practice; it usually takes me two to five minutes. Two to five minutes is good enough to distract your negative thoughts with positive thoughts, and you can do it anywhere. You can practice gratitude while driving, when you're at work taking bathroom breaks, while taking your morning or evening walk, during a shower, or while cooking. So, do not use time as an excuse, Sistergirl. You are worth it.

Please don't confuse gratitude with boasting about what you have or how better you are than others. Use this opportunity to develop compassion for those who are less fortunate than you and use it as a reminder that it's not always about what you don't have, but what you do have and how you can help those less fortunate than you.

"At times, our own light goes out and is rekindled by a spark from another person. Each of us has cause to think with deep gratitude of those who have lighted the flame within us."

-Albert Schweitzer

Don't worry, friend, you aren't alone. I have been there, and I feel you, but if you allow yourself to receive and put in work, I am confident you will feel more in control of your life.

When there is no gratitude, there is no hope, and this becomes an open door for self-pity, which can negatively impact your life. The feeling of hopelessness includes deep valleys of depression. Depression can lead us to a lack of productivity, as you do not feel motivated and then into guilt, which is a dangerous recipe for your health.

While talking about self-pity, it's important to note that pity can be introduced by caring family members and friends who are hurting for you and just really want the best for you. There is a way to avoid this pity.

You can help your family and friends not support a self-pity zone by letting them know that what you really need is their help to solve a situation and not sympathy. I know it comes naturally for people to say things like "poor thing" or "Oh my goodness, you have gone through so much." But if we're not careful, we can soak in these words that are meant for good, which can have a negative impact on us when we begin to believe their words.

> There are no circumstances around you more powerful than the power within you. You are responsible for your life through your consciousness. Racism, sexism, homophobia, and ageism have no power over you unless you believe they do. A belief is the most contagious influence you possess. If you believe in circumstances, they can and will defeat you. If you believe in yourself, you are assured victory. There is a wonderful inner world at work within each of us. It knows no colour, gender, or age. We fuel this inner world with initiative, ingenuity, and a picture in our minds. The world responds and produces according to how we fuel it. If we picture poverty, oppression, failure, disease and doubt, we cannot expect to enjoy wealth, success, and health. When we put the forces of our inner self to work with good thoughts, it will produce according to our system of ideas. If we can keep our inner world clean, fertilize our minds with productive positivity, the powers within will create, with dynamic force, all that we believe is possible. Today I fuel my inner world with positive possibilities.
>
> -Iyanla Vanzant, *Acts of Faith (pg. 168)*

BONUS SECRET

Glenda Standeven

ADVERSITY KNOWS NO BOUNDARIES, UPBRINGING, NOR STATUS, BUT THERE IS A WAY AROUND IT

Your childhood may not have been like mine; in fact, it might have been the opposite of mine. You may have grown up in a well-rounded, loving family, went to school, got great grades, and even married the love of your life; but your life took a turn late in life.

I am honoured and privileged to give you a sneak peek into the life of an amazing powerhouse of a woman who had an amazing upbringing, got married, and had the ideal life with a three-year-old son and a loving husband -- until her life took a turn for the worst. A woman who chose to smile even after losing her entire leg to bone cancer at age thirty-two.

The Inspirational Life Story of a Bone Cancer Survivor chronicles her life adventures before, during, and long after her own cancer journey. In October 2017, her short story "I Just Needed to Say Goodbye" was included in *Chicken Soup for the Soul: Dreams and the Unexplainable*. In June 2018, her second short story "Some Men Run" was included in *Chicken Soup for the Soul - The Miracle of Love*, and a third story "Good Morning Five Toes" was included in the 2019 edition of *Chicken Soup for the Soul – Think Positive and Live Happy*.

Her mission is to share her choosing-to-smile message with everyone she meets and share the many important laugh-worthy life lessons she has learned through not only her own journey, but also her husband's journey with prostate cancer. She's here to remind people of the importance of maintaining a positive attitude of gratitude.

Glenda Standeven is a hemi-pelvectomy amputee and award-winning inspirational speaker.
She is the author of *What Men Won't Talk About and Women Need to Know: A Woman's Perspective on Prostate Cancer* and her autobiography titled *I Am Choosing to Smile.*

IN HER WORDS

Many of us grow up doing our best to cope with adversity on a daily basis, but some of us only fall on hard times later in life. I am one of those people.

I had an idyllic youth - growing up in a loving family, getting good grades, making friends easily, and enjoying perfect health. I was thirty-two years old when my world came crashing down with a diagnosis of bone cancer. The resulting surgery left me disabled with a three-year-old son and a husband I'd only had for five years. To say I was overwhelmed with the turn of events would be an understatement. How do you transition overnight from one body into another? It was like owning a Ferrari one day and then suddenly you're driving a beat up, rusted-out Pinto the next. The treatment for my cancer was an aggressive hemi-pelvectomy surgery that removed my entire right leg, including half my hip and pelvis. I was no longer the fit, able-bodied woman my husband thought he would grow old with.

In some cases, facing adversity at a young age helps to build resiliency. In other instances, it just beats you down until you give up all hope and even getting out of bed becomes an ordeal. Where do we find the strength to carry on?

Family? Definitely! If they are in a position to support and encourage you but, all too often, they are part of the problem.

Friends? Absolutely! Unless they have enough troubles of their own and heaping anything else on their already full plates is not an option.

Faith? Yes! (Unless you have never developed a relationship with a higher power then this is probably not an option either.) I feel I was blessed because I found my strength in all three - faith, family, and friends.

If you're like me, you dislike platitudes. The people who say, "God gave you this disease for a reason" (my God is not that mean); "You're never given more than you can handle" (tell that to the people who commit suicide); "It could always be worse" (sorry, but that doesn't make me feel better). People mean well, but until they have experienced a health crisis or a life crisis for themselves, they really have no idea what to say to comfort and encourage us. I chose to surround myself with people who uplifted me, and I highly recommend this route for anyone struggling to cope with overwhelming challenges. Do not allow people into your circle who suck the courage out of you. I appreciated it when my friends and family would say things like, "Well, this sure sucks, doesn't it? What are you going to do to make it better?" This was putting the power to recover squarely on my shoulders rather than giving it away to someone else to do it for me or making me feel powerless by saying, "Oh you poor thing."

It drives me crazy when people offer me pity instead of empathy. I've learned to tell people outright that I feel very privileged to be alive and not to feel sorry for me. It took a while to become this confident and I remember a time, shortly after my amputation, when I was in the bank waiting in line for a teller. An elderly lady I recognized came up to me and patted me placatingly on the arm saying, "I am so sorry for you, my dear. I just don't know why such bad things happen to such nice people."

The pity fairly oozed from her and it made me wish I could just run away! Instead, I refused to be seen as a person to be pitied, and I drew myself up as tall as my crutches and one leg would allow, raised my eyebrows, and innocently asked, "How did you know I was getting a cold Mrs. B? Is my nose red? I always get a cold this time of year!" The look on her face was priceless. She stammered and stuttered with the realization that I was not about to become an object of pity and, if I wasn't going to feel sorry for myself, nobody else had the right to do that either.

One major breakthrough I had during my journey was discovering that most people are happy to help. I'll never forget going to a cancer workshop a few months after my amputation. During our lunch break, they served a lovely pasta buffet – on paper plates. I was a one-legged lady on crutches, but nobody stepped forward to offer to help me carry my plate. Being new to the world of being disabled, I didn't feel comfortable asking for help, so I tried my best to carry my load of spaghetti and sauce back to my table on my own. Unfortunately, the paper plate was not designed to be carried in one hand and, right over the head of the lady sitting beside me, the plate snapped in half and my load of spaghetti and sauce plopped right on top of her head – and just like that she was wearing a pasta hat! At that moment I wanted to disappear but, bless that lady's forgiving heart, she brushed the spaghetti out of her eyes, looked up at me and smiled as she said, "Well, that wasn't the look I was going for!" We all burst out laughing and I realized two important lessons that day: It is MUCH easier to ask for help than to try to clean up the mess you make trying to do it all yourself and ALWAYS maintain your sense of humour!

Some people think it is a sign of weakness to ask for help. Believe me, it is much more courageous to accept that you need a hand and be brave enough to reach out for it than to suffer longer than necessary trying to reach your goals alone. Please don't ever think that you need to struggle through life on your own. There are health professionals who will guide you to wellness; there are friends who will listen and, if you haven't found one yet, keep looking! But it is not all about receiving help. It is also about giving it!

It took time, but when I was feeling emotionally and physically well enough to give back, I did just that. I joined an Optimist Club, volunteered with the Cancer Society, volunteered with the Terry Fox Foundation, and helped others in any way I could. I became an inspirational speaker talking to kids about the importance of accepting people who look different on the outside. My wonderful husband and I even had another child after my amputation. I worried my hubby wouldn't love me as a one-legged woman, but he told me he didn't marry me for my legs. (Thank goodness he's a boob man!) In a way, my adversity became my strength.

There are so many trials that can defeat us - physical, mental, financial, grief, abuse… In my mind, life is a simple diagram of an old-fashioned well – sometimes we stand in the light at the top of the well, helping those who have fallen in to climb out and sometimes we are the ones at the bottom reaching to those at the top to help lift us. It is all about choices. We can choose to stand in the comfort of the light and just observe the struggles and pain of others without ever reaching out to help. We can choose to stay stuck in the bottom of the well in darkness without lifting our eyes to see the help waiting for us in the light. I am very grateful for the helping hands who lifted me from the well when I'd fallen in. I am equally grateful now to stand in the light and help those who are down by sharing my story and my experiences.

May you always find the courage to lift your eyes to the light and extend your hand in gratitude to those who offer theirs.

My goodness. What an amazing story of strength, grace, determination, and a great attitude through it all. I hope you enjoyed, smiled, and even giggled a little as much as I did as I read Glenda's story. Be sure to connect with her and grab her books on Amazon by searching for her name or book titles.

To book Glenda for an event, contact her at glendastandeven@gmail.com

For more information, visit her website at www.glendastandeven.com

The great late Maya Angelou (an icon, American author, actress, screenwriter, dancer, poet, and civil rights activist) gave what I consider the best advice. She said, "Let gratitude be the pillow upon which you kneel to say your nightly prayer. And let faith be the bridge you build to overcome evil and welcome good."

REFLECTION

Think of three people in your life that you are thankful for, write why you are thankful for them, in detail, and decide on how and when you will show your gratitude to them.

Many people ask me how I can keep a smile on my face and seem unbothered by many life challenges, but the truth is not that I am not bothered. Life will always throw balls and sometimes stones at you, but instead of staring and meditating on those challenges, I meditate on gratitude and that's how I am able to keep a smile on my face.

I appreciate and focus on what I have instead of what's lacking in my life. I embrace the journey of where I am at, where I am going, and I pray and strategically plan as I work to get to where I want to be rather than entertaining the thought of dissatisfaction.

HOW YOU CAN PRACTICE GRATITUDE:

Pray. If you are a believer, pray. You can pray for the sick, the hungry, those mourning a loved one, orphans and widows, as well as those who are hurting, be it physically or emotionally. Give thanks for living another day because not everyone was blessed enough to see this day. You got to be here today; not because you gave anything to deserve it, but because of his grace. When there are more things going wrong than right, it can feel tough to find something to be thankful for, but as you pray for these people, you will realize how rich and blessed you are.

Meditate on positivity. Preferably set a few minutes aside each day to sit down in a non-destructive environment and just close your eyes to reflect on what went well. What made you smile? Who helped you? Who did you help? This can be a person or thing. Think outside the box. You can also write them if that's your preference.

Practice saying thank you often. I can't say this enough. Even if it's a paid service, thank them for doing an amazing job if they did well on your project. Expressing your appreciation of the person's knowledge, skills, and dedication will not only have a positive impact on your life, but it will also have a similar impact on the other person providing the service, which is win-win. How many people do you pay and only get crappy products or services? You let them know how you feel; right? So, why not do the same for those who did a great job? A secret many people don't know is that people are more willing and open to go an extra mile for you if they feel appreciated than when they are being torn apart with ridicule. Being appreciative nurtures your working relationship, which can lead to connections and deals you would have never imagined.

It may seem strange at first to do this exercise, but remember practice and persistence are the mothers of all skills!!!

3

Secret Three
A Little TLC for Your Body, Mind, and Soul

Motivational speaker (my personal all-time favourite) and best-selling author Lisa Nichols said, "So often we take care of everybody and the whole time we're putting ourselves on the back burner. This is the season to 'do you' first."

In a study conducted by Munchery, researchers looked into the everyday lives of 2,000 moms and dads and found that the typical parent has just over thirty minutes to themselves each day after tending to work and parental duties. With the free time almost impossible to come by, many parents polled said they hid from their children to take a breather. A whopping 32 percent of parents don't stop "working" until at least 8:00 p.m. and 24 percent of parents spend over thirty hours every single week directly taking care of their children in addition to other responsibilities and traveling back and forth for children's activities.[3]

Let me confess that it would be very unfair if I did not talk about recharging physically. This is like servicing you; you are the vehicle for everything you do. Without you, none of those things you do will be completed. Right?

Now, I am a visual learner and a lover of simplicity when it comes to understanding things; therefore, we are going to use a very practical, simple example. Take a moment to think about all the valuable possessions you own. What are they? You service them or take extra special care of them, right? Great!

Let's use a car as an example, since it is something many of us own and worry about. We can agree that maintenance is crucial for safety and the vehicle's longevity. We also know if not maintained regularly, the consequences are greater. It can cost hundreds to thousands of dollars to repair. In fact, it can even cost us our lives, to some extent, if we ignore these steps to ensure our vehicle is safe to drive. You and I can agree that it is much cheaper to routinely take it for check-up than having to do major repairs for things we could have avoided (and to avoid this huge expense).

What do we do? We do routine maintenance for our vehicles. We clean them, we change oil, change filters, we check tire pressure, check breaks, we check signals, and lights. We quickly make an appointment with our mechanic when the "check engine" light comes on, even if we just came from the mechanic the same day. Right?

Just like your vehicle, balance is not about burning yourself out 24/7, 365 days a year, and trying to do it all (at all times) simply because you are a single mom. A healthy balance involves prioritizing what matters the most to you, which also aligns with your values and desires.

---

3   See the reference page for a link to the study.

Sistergirl, we have both agreed on some of the reasons why it's very crucial to maintain our vehicles due to the important role they play in our lives. They move us from where we are to where we want to go.

The consequences of not doing a routine check of your body (I don't mean going to the doctor per se) can be great. It is equally imperative, if not more so, to do a heart, mind, and body check-in with yourself, charge your battery before it runs out, do routine maintenance, and look out for that engine light calling for your attention before you breakdown.

Personally, I have experienced burnout and extreme exhaustion and believe me, it's not cool. It is much more than just being very tired. I would shake uncontrollably, avoid everybody, and even a simple noise like a door knock would throw me off. I would yell at my kids and then feel bad and guilty about it. I would sleep all the time, or if not sleeping, I would eat anything that came my way, which often led to weight gain and then self-image sabotage. The list of my burnout experience is long, but you never want to go through it if you haven't. With extreme exhaustion comes decreased motivation and a lack of productivity, feelings of isolation, depression, more work sickness leaves that costs you money, and a reputation that can hinder your promotion opportunities. Irritation also comes, which costs your children and the people around you their joy. It can lead to depletion in children as well. In all honesty, it is awfully hard to be fully present for your child when you are not well.

According to Dr. Danielson[4], "The question I ask mothers is, 'If you were choosing a childcare provider, and you had a choice between someone who seemed stressed, tired, and overwhelmed versus someone who seemed rested, contented, happy and healthy, who would you want for your kids? If you can't do it for yourself, do it for your kids.'"

I want you to look at your body as your favourite or most ideal vehicle that it is; treat it like you would if it was your Ferrari, your Lamborghini, Mercedes Benz, Tesla, Porsche, BMW, or whatever your fantasy car may be. It's unfortunate that most of us treat monetary possessions so much better than we do ourselves – we who are the ultimate holders/drivers that produce or create those possessions. Your body is much more valuable than any of the cars mentioned. I want you to pause and think of your favourite vehicle, jewels, or whatever you

---

4   Dr. Aimee L. Danielson, PhD is a licensed clinical psychologist with specialized training and over fifteen years of experience in Maternal Mental Health and a director of the Women's Mental Health Program at MedStar Georgetown University Hospital. See reference page for more details.

value the most, and think of how you treat it or how you would treat it. Then, do 10x better for your body. Do routine maintenance on it, lookout for the "check engine" light, which indicates exhaustion, and make an appointment with a mechanic, which means to rest, do something fun, treat yourself to go somewhere, something nice, and/or seek professional help.

Life is too short to work extremely hard and not enjoy the fruit of your sweat. I am a big believer of working hard and playing harder. Why do we hustle anyway? I don't know about you, but for me I hustle so I can build a legacy for my children and their children, make a greater impact in the world by contributing what I can, and have a good, comfortable, happy life.

I know the amount of pressure on single parents is sometimes too much, even from the people we love and care about. We are unfortunately misjudged, both intentionally and unintentionally. We get overwhelmed by the never-ending work at home, running after the little ones, feeding them, cooking, cleaning up toys, or keeping the big boys and girls busy with activities. It's so easy to forget ourselves because we feel we are too busy and want to do it all (all the time), or because we don't want to be judged as inadequate or selfish parents. We feel guilty for taking time "away" from our children or we want to keep up with everyone else. However, as demanding as our lives are, it is paramount that we continuously take and carve out time to fuel our minds, souls, and bodies. Take time to be still and reflect and mingle with other adults. Babies are cute to look at and play with, but as much as it is fun and soothing, it can only be so cute and fun for so many hours a day without a break.

Here is a great example of how people we love can sometimes contribute to our lack of self-care or feeling guilty for taking time "away" from our children.

One day, I was tired and just not feeling like myself, and while I can't quite remember what I told my children, I remember a statement from someone present that shocked me. She said, "In parenting, it is not about quantity versus quality." I was offended. I thought about it for a few days, and it took me back to my early years of parenting when I felt like less of a mom. Even though I knew that wasn't her intention, it was far from how I translated it. It affected me for a few days until I took time to go back to the first chapter of this book: self-awareness. I had to acknowledge my situation and give myself permission to operate my family a little differently. I did it in a way I felt was right for me and my children versus trying to keep up with Jones' (what everyone thinks a mother should be like).

It was either I make peace with my way of parenting, as long as I was giving my best, or I beat myself up each time another mom seemed do a better job in my eyes, or I beat myself up each time someone threw me a little jab on my parenting (everyone does the best they know how). I chose to guard my heart, mind, and stood on the truth that only my children and I know about my parenting.

I had to realize this woman had, as her kids were growing up, someone to give her a break when she needed. She probably wasn't juggling two jobs to put food on the table or maybe was just home with her kids as a stay-at-home mom. Please note that I am not encouraging you to not maximize your time with your children or neglect them; in fact, I advise you to spend every chance you get with them, but equally take time for yourself to refuel for them!

Unfortunately, as single parents, it is a reality that we often must parent in quality versus quantity mode, and I want you to know that it is perfectly fine. As single parents, almost everything takes double time and double effort because we are trying to split ourselves into so many people, things, and places all at once. We don't have another person to ask for a break from when we are feeling down and just need a little time alone (me-time). Wherever we leave a mess is where we will find it, and yes, we get a little more irritated than a home with two parents in most cases. It's okay. If it means letting kids spend time alone watching TV while you get your break/nap, then that's how it is as long as they are safe. I would rather spend one hour of quality time creating good memories versus spending five hours yelling at the top of my lungs because I am frustrated, overwhelmed, or mad at their dad for the sake of quantity. That does not help me or them much.

There are many simple, fun ways we can recharge and/or maintain our mental, emotional, and physical wellbeing without needing childcare each time or spending crazy amounts of money. I will share a few of those.

I want to be clear that I am not a medical doctor, a psychiatrist, or any kind of mental health professional. I am just a single mummy who tried many tips and tricks to help me balance my roles between being a mummy and a professional in the corporate world. Juggling two jobs and giving your goals a fair shot while still prioritizing your self-care needs is doable!

For me to accomplish these things, I must be happy, healthy, and alive! I must value myself first and demonstrate that to myself by paying attention and listening to my body. I must work for it because I am in a driver's seat of my own happiness. No one knows when they will die, but I want to give a great shoot at longevity, and when I die young, I want to die happy and full of love.

Since you are the driver of your life, you must decide which direction you want to steer your vehicle. Be intentional about putting yourself first and show up for yourself before everybody else. You can't be busy taking care of your children, work, friendships, businesses, and everything else, and put yourself last when, ultimately, you are the key element to making magic happen.

Sistergirl, this took me a long time to master because I tend to feel like I am a magician with a magic wand who can take everyone's pain away. But I understand that even God, who created people, lets them feel the pain and find their own answers first. Otherwise, there would be no sorrow, death, or single motherhood.

Some of these tips may not work for you if your children are very little, but I found them very helpful. Putting things like cereal, bread, and other easy-to-grab snacks within my children's reach saved me big-time, especially on those days when I wasn't feeling well. Teaching them some house chores at a noticeably young age helped (start involving them now if they can talk and stand). There are tons of helpful ideas on Pinterest that you can use as a guideline, but every child is different. You know your child best, so decide what you feel is accurate to teach your child based on their age.

Below are a few other options that I have explored. You can choose from this list, mix and match, and make it your own. Please don't try to do it all at once, otherwise you may get overwhelmed, become frustrated, and eventually quit. I highly suggest you start with one or two!

- Take vitamins and eat healthy. (You do not need to be a vegetarian if that's not your choice.)

- Meditate. Mindfulness helps us calm down. This can be done anywhere, including the shower, lying on your bed, or whenever you get a chance to just be still and breathe deeply without interruption.

- Exercise or stretch. You don't need to be a fitness guru or have a shredded body. I sometimes have to do mine on the bathroom or kitchen floor with the vent on to make sure I don't wake anyone. Put your child in a stroller for a nice evening or morning stroll in nature. Follow a YouTube video on your phone or laptop. Have a dance or pass-the-ball party while running in circles, and you can make it into a game with your kids if they are up (blast the music on your TV). And if your pocket permits, it's even better if you can join a fitness centre with daycare onsite options (I loved Zumba). I highly suggest you get ready everything you would need the night before and leave them on your dining chair or in the bathroom to avoid waking everybody up.

- Have fun alone in the comfort of your home. Sistergirl, shake that booty; shake what your mama gave you. Whip that beautiful long hair back and forth! You can do this while your child is in a playpen, playing with toys, watching TV, playing in the backyard, or you can wake up earlier than your child. Even ten minutes makes a big difference.

- Connect with your tribe (other single mamas). Meet either online or in-person. I think it's much better in-person because once you establish a good relationship and see that you have similar values in your parenting (can build trust), then you can take turns babysitting for each other to get a break or hangout while kids are having play dates. It doesn't have to be only with single moms; even non-single moms can be your tribe because you still have something in common. This saved me when I first started working because one of my friends and I had opposite schedules.

- Start a routine. I highly suggest a routine of some sort, especially a bedtime routine for your child. This gives you time to have a glass of wine to yourself or a cup of tea in peace. This is not set in stone as we know life happens, and we can't always stick to it, but it's great to have it in place so you both then have a guideline and know what to expect. I am thankful my spiritual sister introduced me to this concept a few years ago before she even became a mom herself! It has surely served me well. Even if the child is still a baby, try to get them on a routine so they will grow into it. Bonus: This also comes in handy when you start dating because you then have time to have some romantic time on the phone or cuddle!

Now, those were some of the everyday maintenance I have tried. Do what is best for you. Just do something! You can't get by with only the few minutes you manage to snatch during the day. You deserve better!

In this next section, I will walk you through some boosters! Some ways I recharge. Remember the point here is to balance parenting, social life, our hobbies, work life, other life demands, and our overall health. We want to be able to understand and cope with our emotions, create healthy relationships, keep healthy, and feel energized. We want to find our purpose in life, and not make parenting seem like the worst chore in the world or a death sentence -- when in essence, it's the best and the most rewarding job anyone can ever do!

I keep saying I can apply for all the jobs, I can decide on which ones to apply for, but I didn't apply to have my children or decide the type of children I wanted. I'm so glad the man upstairs (God) made the epic choice for me. I am honoured that he valued me enough and trusted me with the most precious gifts in the world, and I am going to ensure that I do a damn good job by taking care of myself first so I can spread that love to my children!

By the way, my kids think I am insane because I am the kind of mummy that will gift myself on all holidays that I would have liked someone to acknowledge me. I gift myself on Valentine's Day, Christmas, I go big on my birthdays, and anytime in-between when I feel like it and am able.

Honey, you set the rhythm of how you want to be treated by treating yourself that way first! Imagine if you had your dream guy who is so loving, he is hot and sexy (in your eyes), that your smile magically becomes brighter when you see him walk through the door, and you feel like you own the world when he hugs you tight. But he never shows up, sends a gift, or even calls you on your special occasions. How long will he be really that cute for? How much longer will you be in love with him for? Will his absence and lack of acknowledgment on your special occasions truly make you feel like the queen he claims you are to him? I am not sure about you, but for me the answer is absolutely not! But wait a minute, Sis, why is it a big deal that he shows up for you while you don't even show up for yourself? Something to think about!

So, let's dive in and get to the nuggets!

STEPS TO ALLOW "ME-TIME" TO RECHARGE

1. Make a list of things you like to do (your hobbies/self-care regimes).

2. Look at your already set schedules such as work, prayer meetings, kid's activities, and anything you do on a regular basis.

3. As you make your to-do list for the week, make an appointment with yourself, your girlfriends, or your partner, if you have one. This may need a little extra planning if you have small children that can't be left alone for a few hours, as you may have to check in with your babysitter to see what their availability is first.

4. After you have looked at what makes you happy, figured out your schedule, made an appointment with yourself or whoever your date is going to be, and arranged for childcare, then get sexy or comfortable and go have a blast!

Sistergirl, you may be thinking, *She is insane. How can I possibly do that when the house is dirty?* I get you Sistergirl, but who cares? So what? It's your home and tomorrow is another day, but today is your date and that's what's up. I am not encouraging you to live in an unhealthy environment, but if it's just a few dishes and few toys, who cares. As long as they don't stink, it's fine.

I know that the demands on single parents never ends, but we too are humans and very much deserve all the happiness the universe has to offer. Okay, so you may be saying, "But Rebecca, I don't have time." None of us has time, girlfriend; we prioritize and make time! And you can, too! Utilize your family, friends, high school students looking for pocket money, and your fellow mamas! "Someday soon" or "maybe when things get better" isn't enough. As parents, we have to prioritize our mental well-being as much as we prioritize our children's activities. Would you ever miss your child's hockey or soccer game? Absolutely not -- unless there is an emergency. Our mental well-being is equally, if not more so, important and must be prioritized.

You might be saying, "But Rebecca, are you crazy? I can't even pay my bills. Where will I get money from?" Let me ask you a question. When was the last time you drove through for a meal or coffee? When last did you buy another pair of shoes? Can you cut back and go for basic cable instead of paying for the premium package when you don't watch all those channels? Can you shop around to switch your phone plan to a cheaper one? When was the last time you bought toys for the kids while you complained of too many toys in the house? I know we mamas tend to overdo it on toys. Can you perhaps pick up two extra hours at work that week to fund your date? It's okay to outsource services. I used to have a lady come clean for me every two weeks for $60 each time because I hated cleaning my own home but loved my job. I also paid a lot of friend's children to babysit for me because it was so important to get time to myself, even if that meant just napping without kids knocking on my door ten times in one minute. Both my families are my rock stars. Even to this day they take my kids now and then to give me a break, which I am grateful for.

Remember your date does not need to be expensive, nor does it even need to be the traditional kind of date. You set your rhythm -- you do you! You can have a picnic, go for a road trip, go camping, or send the kids to your parents for the weekend. You can go watch a movie with a friend. (I always fall asleep no matter how interesting the movie is. My kids still can't get over that I slept through almost the entire *Black Panther* movie, at a movie theatre, in the front row, and with my son on my lap.) You can also go to some kind of class, like a Spinning class. Be your authentic self because no one knows you and your needs better. When you take care of yourself, you're a better person for yourself, your children, and it's easier for others to be and want to be around you.

I don't mean to scare you, but if you do not prioritise yourself and make time for you to be still, rejuvenate, or do whatever makes you happy -- be ready to pay the price. Work never ends and no man or woman has ever said they have too much money. No matter how much money rich people have, they always want more.

And yes, do your best for you and your kids in the way that you know how, and leave the rest to the Lord. Your inner-peace and happiness are a requirement to becoming a better mom to your children, Sistergirl. Quit the illusion of perfect parenting or you will eventually feel more overwhelmed, exhausted, and frustrated to which you may then become impatient and burned out.

The freedom we are looking for is the freedom to be ourselves -- to express ourselves. But if we look at our lives, we see that most of the time we do things just to please others and just to be accepted by others, rather than living our lives to please ourselves. That is what has happened to our freedom.

And we see in our society and all the societies around the world, that for every 1,000 people, 999 are completely domesticated. The worst part is that most of us are not even aware that we are not free. There is something inside that whispers to us that we are not free, but we do not understand what it is, and why we are not free.

The following is an excerpt from a book called *The Four Agreements* depicting the concept of freedom or lack thereof of people:

> The problem with most people is that they live their lives and never discover that the Judge and the Victim rule their mind, and therefore, they don't have a chance to be free. The first step toward personal freedom is awareness. We need to be aware that we are not free in order to be free. We need to be aware of what the problem is in order to solve the problem. Awareness is always the first step because if you are not aware, there is nothing you can change. If you are not aware that your mind is full of wounds and emotional poison, you cannot begin to clean and heal the wounds and you will continue to suffer. There is no reason to suffer. With awareness you can rebel and say, "This is enough!" You can look for a way to heal and transform your personal dream. The dream of the planet is just a dream. It is not even real. If you go into the dream and start challenging your beliefs, you will find that most of the beliefs that guided you into the wounded mind are not even true. You will find that you suffered all those years of drama for nothing. Why? Because the belief system that was put inside your mind is based on lies. That is why it is important for you to master your own dream; that is why the Toltecs became dream masters. Your life is the manifestation of your dream; it is an art. And you can change your life anytime if you aren't enjoying the dream. Dream masters create a masterpiece of life; they control the dream by making choices. Everything has consequences and a dream master is aware of the consequences. To be Toltec is a way of life. It is a way of life where there are no leaders and no followers, where you have your own truth and live your own truth. A Toltec becomes wise, becomes wild, and becomes free again.
>
> -DON MIGUEL RUIZ, *The Four Agreements, THE TOLTEC PATH TO FREEDOM, Breaking Old Agreements (pg. 6)*

BONUS SECRET

Sabrina Runbeck

Life is hard and sometimes we feel helpless and stuck or frustrated, not because we aren't smart or work hard as others, but because we neglect some important areas of our lives. The most important asset we possess -- is us! It's also okay to acknowledge that you don't know everything, and you may need help to see things on a bigger scale.

Because I have understood this for myself, I have brought in my good friend to provide some of her personal insight with you. She is someone who I have had a pleasure to spend six weeks one-on-one training with during my book journey in order to hold myself accountable and balanced as I took on this daunting task.

I call her the queen of gaining clarity! I knew why I wanted to write this book, but I was stuck on how to "put my 'why' down on the paper." She also made sure I came through with my deadlines, made time for my children, my self-care, kept a great attitude, and energized me through it! She was always ready to listen, ready to brainstorm, and I love that she just does not talk. There was always a different practical exercise after each session, which was fantastic!

Sabrina Runbeck is a Cardiothoracic surgery PA, a public health practitioner, and a peak performance coach/speaker who empowers ambitious young professionals, especially those working in healthcare, to become confident leaders. Her mission is to support these people so they can be BOTH a powerhouse in their career and feel passionate about life again without feeling overwhelmed, underappreciated, or undervalued.

IN HER WORDS

Four years ago, at about eight o'clock in the morning, I was exhausted, had barely slept, had a fever of 101 degrees, my body felt weak, and my hands were having cramps… the problem was that I had my hands inside of a patient's open chest while attempting to finish performing an open-heart surgery … while knowing I would not have a break for at least another five hours.

Then the beeper, that had been paging me all night, just went off again while we were operating. This noise just made my exhaustion harder to hide. One nurse took pity on me and slipped cough drops and Dayquil under my mask to keep me going.

Unfortunately, when I woke up the next day, I was covered with night sweats and could barely get out the bed. I had to call my boss to take a sick day. He responded, "Why didn't you tell me this earlier? Okay, just don't make a habit out of this." Wait! Am I inconveniencing *him*?

I was so frustrated at that time because in any professional setting, we value our clients with compassion and respect, but we were not treating our teammates and ourselves with these values.

As someone who always wanted to be ambitious and driven, I used, "Yes, I got this," as my default. I kept pushing myself to the limit, hardly ever allowed myself to take a day off even when I was sick. So, I took on yet another consultation, did another procedure, and reviewed another chart, but I was never seemed to be doing enough.

I then questioned if I was ever going to be enough. These distracting yeses take away our precious time, energy, and sanity.

We all have worked ridiculously hard to get to where we are right now. We didn't do it just to hate every moment we spend working, or to just give up and jump ship to a different field because we felt underappreciated or undervalued.

I believe that with the right system, us young, ambitious professionals can be *both* - powerhouses in our careers and passionate people in life.

So, I went back to my roots in neuroscience and public health; I dug out my own thesis on self-care & self-efficacy, tried different self-lead programs (because my pride thought I could just do everything myself), and realized that without a one-on-one coach, I was not seeing my own blind spots.

Finally, after years of struggling, I coached myself out of constant exhaustion, and created a system that turned my life around.

I'm Sabrina Runbeck, a surgical PA and a peak performance coach. Now, I love working in surgery again and empowering other young professionals with demanding careers, like healthcare, to have a life full of "Heck YES" so they can start their day feeling excited, while rising as leaders to truly feeling powerful and passionate again.

Let me share with you the three steps that have worked for me.

3-STEPS TO SELF-CARE

#1) Reboot your mental immunity

Our primitive brain is constantly scanning for negative things and creating automatic negative thoughts to protect ourselves.

We can stop these negative thoughts from bombarding our mind by building mental immunity, so we can conquer all unpredicted or unseen roadblocks from our internal and external sabotages.

Everyone has unpredictable roadblocks. The "I'm positive I can" attitude generates the power, energy and skills needed to overcome them.

It's unusual for many of us just to wake up, jump out of bed, and start blowing our own horn and cheering ourselves on. Write down three things. Say one good thing about yourself out loud every morning to begin the day on a good note. It might feel awkward at first, but soon you'll feel the power that positivity can bring there.

#2) Redefine your motivations

Make less time for "busy" work and spend more time focusing on what lights you up. For example, I get up every morning at 5:00 a.m. so I can have a power hour to warm up my body by practicing yoga, boosting my mind by listening to a motivational podcast, and check in with myself to start my day energized.

Say "no" to vagueness, so you can dream big and achieve more. Any time you are wavering between choices, unclear on the ultimate goal, or do things just because someone asked you to without being connected to its mission, you are wasting your time being busy. You are too vague and aren't clear about your goals, which should guide your choices. People cannot read our minds. When we have a clear purpose and can explain it well for others, then they are likely to support our mission and help us achieve those results. I would suggest, before diving into any projects, write a one-sentence purpose statement.

#3) Recreate micro vacations daily

Take micro mental vacations to reboot your energy, otherwise you won't last long in your passion career. Practicing micro mental vacations, and when done correctly, allows you to instantly bring back your energy, focus, and calmness to your mind. Knowing that our optimal concentration span is thirty to sixty minutes, adding these exercises in between your major tasks allows you to get things done a lot faster than pushing yourself to the limit.

There are many types of micro mental vacations exercises on YouTube. You have to play around to see which ones may benefit you the most. In the meantime, hop on and try one to see how you feel. You may feel lighter? Calmer? More focused? Energized? Or a combination of these. Wouldn't you want to feel that way all the time instead of letting mental chatters bombard your mind?

The 3-step process we just discussed is part of your self-care. Taking care of ourselves is a form of creating influence. When we can control our own behaviours and influence ourselves, then we are truly living in a charged life by focusing on our growth first and not default into a comfortable life that becomes complacent and boring. If we cannot influence our own mind, decisions, and behaviour, then how can we expect to influence and create better outcomes for others?

Having a life full of "Heck YES" requires conscious intentions.

Be a good influence to yourself so you feel alive and energized for making positive impacts in the lives of others. I used to work over eighty hours per week and felt exhausted all the time; now I found ways to feel energized during a five-hour surgery. I used to get up and rush out of the door, now I wake up and listen to my energy playlist. I used to miss my workout classes, but now I can squat 225 pounds, which means I could squat with Lebron James across my shoulders. I used to complain about my situation, now I live a life full of meaning and excitement without compromising my well-being, all while using my 3-step system to empower other young professionals to do the same. Find something that you love and enjoy in place of the negative one that you don't necessarily enjoy.

From the minute I realized my tried-and-true system could save someone from binge-watching YouTube for hours or reading hundreds of self-help books without making any progress, I knew this was the right path for me.

What I didn't expect were the incredible relationships that I would build along the way with so many amazing individuals. People who deeply care about the success of those whom they serve, who also want to stand up to set good examples for their loved ones, their colleagues, and ultimately for themselves.

You can be both powerful and passionate… where you can overcome any mental roadblocks keeping you from success.

You can be both powerful and passionate… where you are no longer are distracted by mundane busy work and focused only on the things that matter.

You can be both powerful and passionate… where you feel energized from the moment you wake up to the time you go to bed.

Join me and together we can create a life where you can be both powerful and passionate!

Wow, Sistergirl, those were some helpful nuggets Sabrina just poured out! If you are feeling stuck and are interested in connecting with Sabrina, then you can learn more about gaining a clear and energized mind, and how to have a powerful and passionate life, through her six-week 1-on-1 program or join her community for a six-month mastermind. She will tailor to your needs and will help you move from feeling overwhelmed, undervalued, and underappreciated, to leading an energized, poised, and enriched life.

Connect with Sabrina here:
- SabrinaRunbeck.com/hello
- Instagram.com/SabrinaRunbeck
- LinkedIn.com/in/SabrinaRunbeck
- FB.me/SabrinaRunbeck
- SabrinaRunbeck.com

4

Secret Four
Forgive Faster to Heal Sooner

I whole-heartedly believe you must let go of the past to receive the present! It is too great of a burden to carry around the pain, the betrayals, the disappointments, and the anger caused by another person, who is enjoying their life while you are busy mourning and killing yourself slowly. This individual you are carrying around on your shoulders probably doesn't even care whether you are hurt or not. It has been proven that the act of forgiveness frees not only you, but also improves your health by lowering your blood pressure and reducing your anxiety and stress levels. It also improves your mental health and self-esteem.

I have learned that forgiveness isn't just something nice to do. It is a necessity to free myself from the bondage of anger, resentment, and hate, which are blockages to my healing. I must forgive -- not because the other person asked for forgiveness, but to give my soul peace. I have to constantly and consciously make a choice to release and detach from every single person, situation or thing that doesn't serve a purpose or have a positive impact on my life regardless of how hard it might be. Sistergirl, if it doesn't serve a divine purpose in my life, it equally doesn't have a place in my life, either.

Food for thought: Would you put your fresh groceries in the fridge without cleaning out the rotten or expired items from over a month or a year ago? It would rot and stink. It wouldn't look as organized, right? Same thing goes for your heart.

Sistergirl! Why would you want to miss out on these amazing benefits, plus more, and risk losing your life early -- leaving your beautiful children alone in this big crazy world because of someone else's mistake or misery?

Forgiving requires intention, humility, boldness, and even putting on a pair of big-girl pants at times, but it is a necessary step and an important one. If you genuinely want to enjoy yourself today and tomorrow, you must make a conscious decision to release them and let go of negative feelings about them. While there is no justifiable reason to mistreat another person, it is important that you understand that you aren't perfect either, and if you are truly working on healing and living abundant life, then try not to question if that person is worthy or deserving of your forgiveness. Do your part of releasing them and let God do the rest. Forgiveness sets you free from anger and bitterness and makes room for the greater things to flow into your life. It is imperative you acknowledge this life is a mystery, and because it is a mystery, we do not always understand why people do the things they do to their fellow beings. However, as someone who has experienced many heartbreaks and deep disappointments, I have come to observe that in most cases people's acts and behaviours reflect their own thoughts, hurts, or beliefs. People cannot give what they don't have or do what they don't know.

Everything has a reason, including those senseless acts, and because everything has a reason, in most cases it is not about us -- but about them. While we can't look into their hearts/minds to know their reasoning or force our beliefs and reasons on them, we can decide on what to accept, decline, keep, or release. Understanding this has truly helped me on my healing journey.

I have also come to realize and encountered three types of people who intentionally hurt others:

The first group of people are those who have been hurt and haven't properly dealt with their own past trauma/disappointments. My family, as well as one of my exes in the story that I will share in the coming chapters, fell into this category.

The second set are those miserable people with low self-esteem, who are intimidated by your greatness, and those who see you as a threat and want to ensure they bring you down to their level. Remember Michelle Obama's famous phrase? "When they go low, we go high!" Yesss, that's what I'm talking about, girl! These people are so low that they can't stand lifting your head to look at your greatness; promise me you won't fall into that trap. Stay high, mama, you got this!

And the third group of people are simply bad people. Now, we don't know their reasons why they think it is okay to hurt others, but we do know that everyone thinks and processes things differently. So, I am sure they too have their own way of looking at and processing things. However, no matter what their reasoning may be, DO NOT allow yourself to be their victim.

Sistergirl, allow me to share with you some of my toughest experiences from some of the above categories and an example of the forgiving I have had to do to gain my peace and sanity.

In 2017, I met a person in the third category. I met a man who told me I could profit from the stock market, but he scammed me, instead. In mere seconds, I lost $15,776.18 USD. This person didn't care that I was a single mom, that I had a great vision, or that I had already spent money on this vision -- despite the many emails I sent pleading to the company and my account manager explaining why I needed this money.

I had to forgive them, even without them asking for forgiveness, and let go so I could open my heart for whatever the universe offered next. I was forced to shift, and this phase was especially hard because even my car quit on me around the same time. I moved so many hours away from my family to start my African clothing boutique. It was going to be named ALAF, which stood for Africa's Legacy & Aspiration Fashion.

This boutique was a project I had started as part of my healing process after ending my relationship with my best friend, who I had to let go for my children's safety. It had been my escape and a safe space to be creative and connect with myself through different beautiful colours and meanings. I had been working on it for many months. I was fully invested and so passionate about it. I was extremely excited to see it come to life because it was meant to inspire young African people in diaspora to embrace both their Canadian and African cultures through the use of combining African vibrant materials, which holds so much meaning from our ancestors, into Western styles that appeal to young people.

I had spent a lot of money on samples in different countries. I had spent nearly $5,000 on a business plan and research; I had spent many sleepless nights working on it, and I had put in so much of my heart and sweat into it.

Like many people, I had a vision, but didn't have the money. I used my credit cards and borrowed more money from my family, along with whatever bit I had.

I decided to join TR Binary Options (TradeRush) to try to "profit" as much as I could, but I got scammed (couldn't withdraw the money). I planned to put my profits into this business.

I spent many days and hours on the phone and made trips to the police station, but unfortunately, there was nothing the police or anybody could do about it. It all disappeared in the blink of an eye. The loss put me in a great financial strain, and I felt so much shame as I had been actively marketing this business all over my social media. The person in charge of my account suddenly disappeared and that was the end of it. My project and plans had to shift in a different direction.

The practice of forgiveness is not a one-time act; it is ongoing for as long as you live. Forgiveness is not just for when you understand why or when it doesn't sting. Forgiveness is for when you want to be free!

My next example was one of my most recent practices in forgiveness, and probably the hardest one in my adulthood, was a relationship in which I had to end in a matter of seconds. It honestly ended like lightning, and to this day, when I think about it, I am still in shock.

In February 2018, I was in an incredibly happy place all around. I was rebuilding my life, just less than one year after losing my money to Binary Options Trading, from not being able to start my clothing business as initially planned. Towards the end of 2017, I had been introduced to an opportunity in financial services, and I was pumped, I was on fire, and I was just going hard at it. I started doing joint ventures with some of my close friends, including having live guests on my Facebook to reach a greater audience. I decided to do a live video with one of my good friends who is an amazing and well-known DJ in the Kitchener-Waterloo region. I am not sure if you know, but when you are a guest on someone's live Facebook, your friend's guests see the video as well, which was the entire reason for joint ventures to reach a greater audience.

One of the people watching was one of the DJ's friends, a young man named Charlie. Charlie started going wild commenting on the live video, on my pictures and really took an interest in my profile, but I did not think much of it. At the time nothing got my attention unless it was my children, friends, family, or business. Charlie started messaging me requesting to talk, but I was too busy and too invested in my business that I did not have time for small talk. So guess what? Charlie was smart and understood that the only way to get my full attention was to request "more information" about the business.

The city the DJ and Charlie lived in was where my biological family lived, while I lived about five hours away. Through our "more information" conversation and getting to know him, I had mentioned to him about my family being in the area and my plans to come see them in a month's time. I offered for Charlie to meet with one of my business partners in the area to learn more, to attend an information session, and to get to know a little more about the business in person. I felt this was good, so he could make better informed decisions. But he insisted that he would wait until I came down to visit the family, as he didn't trust other people, and preferred to meet with me versus my business partner.

After my efforts to convince him without luck, I told him I understood and would let him know when I was in the area. The month passed by and I was just so busy that I couldn't make it down. I again suggested he meet with my business partner, which he outright refused. He offered to come and meet me in my city instead. I continued to refuse, another month went by, and I eventually told him that if he wanted to come, he could come; however, he had better not expect me to give him a place to sleep or food to eat and should make those arrangements on his own. Charlie agreed that he would pay for his hotel and food during his stay in my city. He bought his plane ticket and came.

Fast forward, Charlie joined me in business, made more trips to my city, and we started talking often for many hours. A few months went by and the next thing I knew, I had fallen into liking him, which was his initial plan. I figured it was okay since he had two children and I had three. We soon discovered that we had both gone through some unpleasant situations and wanted to settle.

In a matter of a few months, Charlie ended up moving to my city. We had what I would call a noticeably short, beautiful relationship. He was great and caring; he loved and respected my children. He really got along with them so well, which won my heart to another level and swept me off my feet, but what I didn't know was that the feeling would be short-lived.

Sistergirl, on July 4, 2019, my world shattered. It came down crashing in full speed. I cried, I felt disgusted, I felt used, lost, and really confused. I wondered if this was my life or a movie playing in my eyes.

The following led to this breakdown:

Charlie had been acting a bit strange the last few days by drinking more, unnecessarily lying to me about small things, and getting angry when I went to do my nails and my hair. He was really getting irritated about very minor things and acting a little insecure with my self-care routines. But I turned a blind eye on these red flags. It got so much worse that I found myself getting on my knees to apologize, which was unlike me. I found myself feeling very bothered by his anger. It felt unbearable to see him unhappy or not being able to talk, play, and laugh with him as usual (he quickly noted these behaviours and really maximized on them/took advantage of it).

When I initially met with Charlie, he did not know how to drive, so we immediately started driving lessons and got his license process started. I also remember asking him, "Now that you are the head of the family, what is your vision for us? Where do you see us in five years from now?" Through this conversation, we decided it was a good idea for him and our family if he went to school to open up doors/more options. He listened to my advice, eventually applied and was accepted to a nearby college into a personal support worker program. He didn't like school as much but was committed to getting this done so we could eventually have a baby, and then I would go back to school or into business full-time.

Because he didn't have a car, we used my car. He would drop me off at work and pick me up. This way he could use the car to go to school/placement or wherever he needed to go.

On June 21, 2019, Charlie did not show up to pick me up as usual. I called many times with no response and instead he texted me twenty-two minutes later informing me that he was somewhere and would not be coming to pick me up nor coming home for the night. He suggested I take an Uber home.

Charlie knew I did not have a credit card (I had buried them) or a Visa debit with me as I was working on becoming debt free and using only cash as much as possible. I reminded him of this and his response was, "Give me the address and I will order Uber for you." I did not respond to this text. My co-worker eventually paid for me with her credit card, and I gave her cash. I got home and as he had said in his text, he was not home and did not come home that night. I was angry and confused as there was no explanation of where he was, what he was doing, or why?

Generally, when I am angry, I give silent treatments; I can't stand the fights back and forth with words. I did not talk to him for days or ask him where he was.

On June 26, as I was getting ready to take to the road for my brother's graduation that would take place on the following day (27th), Charlie requested to talk for the first time since the incident of him not showing up. He said he had something he wanted to tell me.

I told him, "I am all ears."

He sobbed, begged for forgiveness, and gave me crappy lies like, "That day you responded something rude to me when I was dropping you off at work, and I was so upset that I decided to drive around the city all night."

I knew these were lies and far from the truth because we didn't argue even one bit that day nor did I show any signs of unhappiness; in fact, we had spent the morning celebrating my daughter's graduation, which had happened that exact same day (before I went to work). In my mind, I thought he perhaps had gone to Montreal to his best friend's place as he had done it before (his place is two hours away from home); maybe, he decided to lie to me because he knew I didn't like him driving long distance with a G1 license, which does not permit him on the highway or to even drive alone, especially in the night. Not only was my insurance at stake if he got caught, but his life was at stake, since he had only been driving for few months. My second thought was maybe he went out drinking with his friends and perhaps he did not want to drive home drunk or tell me that's what he was doing.

He continued to beg for forgiveness and requested that I not share the incident of him not showing up to pick me up or not sleeping at home.

I asked him, "Why ask for an apology now?" I wondered, *Why on the same day I travel to my family? Why lie to me again about why?* His response was that he wanted me to travel happy and not look sad in front of my family. I accepted his apology, we hugged, I promised not to tell the family, and we moved past that. I did not believe him, but I just wanted my "family" back and had missed the laughter in the house. The kids and I took to the road to celebrate my brother's graduation, and the plan was to spend the weekend there and go back home on Sunday night. We wanted to allow ourselves enough time with the family because both my biological and spiritual family would be there.

On a Saturday evening, I kept feeling something turning in my stomach and an extraordinarily strong gut asked me to head home immediately. I kept fighting it and playing it cool, but it was too strong to ignore. I went into my spiritual parent's basement where they had a setup for me to sleep and laid down for a nap. When I got up, I was 100 percent convinced to head home and that's exactly what I did. I video called Charlie and we talked and laughed, but I did not tell him what I was feeling or that I was coming home.

I packed all my belongings immediately, packed my children into the car, and told the family I was heading home. My family didn't understand, and I really couldn't explain what was going on in my stomach. I don't even remember what I told them, but I can remember them seeming confused. He called me around 12:47 a.m. to say good night and told me he was "going to bed" to which I then pulled over to speak to him, but I did not tell him I was on the road coming home. We drove all night and arrived home around 4:30 a.m. My brother lived nine to ten hours away from us.

When we got home, we left all the belongings in the car and tip-toed upstairs to surprise "daddy" with being home early. To our surprise, all the rooms were empty. We looked in the basement, called and looked everywhere, and daddy was nowhere to be found in the house. So, I told the kids that he was probably out with friends and everything is okay. My kids took my word and went to bed. After putting them in bed, I went and hid all our shoes in the closet, moved my car far away to a visitor's parking where he could not see it if he were coming, I freshened up, and off to bed I went.

I couldn't sleep. I could see he was online on WhatsApp, so I messaged him and told him to call me. I told him, "I am up. I can't sleep." He did not respond. I called, and he did not pick up the phone. So, I waited until about 6:00 a.m. to message him again, this time wishing him a good morning and asking him to call me when he "wakes up."

He did not call me back or message me, and the entire time he was online. Around 6:40 a.m., he walked into our bedroom in his dressy white shirt hanging (untucked) out of his black pants and the tie was the same one he was wearing the day prior when we video called. To his surprise, I was in bed at home, not ten hours away. He was shocked, looked scared, but kept calm. He immediately came to lay on my back (I was lying on my tummy), asking me, "Cherie, when did you come home? What happened to come early? Why did you not say you were coming home?"

I told him I was not interested in any conversation and to move off me. I slept and he slept, but around 10:00 a.m., he woke up to return the unknown red car that he had arrived in. (I went to look through the kid's bedroom window that faced our parking lot when he got up, then went back to bed.)

When he came back from dropping off the car, I asked him whose car that was, and he told me it was one of his friend's car. I believed him because I did not know what car that friend drove. Besides, I wasn't suspecting him of anything other than over-drinking and hanging out with a wrong crowd of young boys. Around 11:30 a.m., I woke up and called one of my girlfriends to go out for lunch, just to distract my mind, but I did not tell her what had happened.

Fast forward, the next few days were a living hell. I gambled away thousands of dollars (some mine and some loans), he drank himself to the point of vomiting in bed, and the once loving, charming Charlie became my nightmare. We became on and off while living under the same roof. It is fair to say we had an unusual attraction for one another that we knew, by the rate our relationship was going, the end was near -- but we both were not ready or willing to give up. With all the madness and unusual sadness, I developed a very unusual cough and fever on July 1st. I bought fever and cough medication, but it did not change a single thing. It got worse on the evening of July 3rd, while I was at work. My co-worker recommended a medication that worked for him when he had had a similar, stubborn cough. I called Charlie and requested that he buy it for me on his way to pick me up, which he did. When he came to pick me up, he seemed a bit worried about something, and a bit off, but he kept calm. I had a very high fever, terrible headache, and was shivering.

When we got inside the house, he told me to get to bed, and that he had to work on his police check (apply online) for a new position he had just been offered in the new field he was graduating from. I got ready and got into bed. A few minutes later he came to ask me for my phone. I told him where it was, pointing at it. I had plugged it in to charge because the battery was low. He reached for it, turned it on, and asked me to put in my password. I asked him what he needed it for, but he responded that he needed to read instructions for my medication. Now, the instructions for medication are usually on the bottle, plus his phone had data and Wi-Fi just like mine did, as well as the computer he was using for his police check application. I did not want to question too much, so I let him do his thing on my phone and slept. Besides, I had nothing to hide, so I let him dig in.

He went back downstairs again and did not come back to bed until after 2:00 a.m. He looked very worried, unenergetic, and each time I asked him if he was okay, he put on a fake smile and forced his mouth on my forehead to kiss it.

The night went by and morning came (I honestly don't think he even slept that day), which was the very fateful day. It was July 4, 2019. We were expecting one of his good friends from the USA to come celebrate the 4th of July with us, but he unfortunately had to cancel the last minute.

Charlie woke up exceedingly early and was on the phone doing what looked like texting back and forth, while sitting down on the bed beside where I was lying down. Again, I am not one to go into a man's phone and honestly, after all these red flags, it still did not come close to my mind that he could be having an affair. I woke up a few minutes past 7:20 a.m., and we were just in bed talking, laughing, and playing like many couples do (our relationship had become on and off in a span of two to three weeks).

A few minutes before 8:00 a.m. my phone rang. He quickly answered the phone and only said, "Hello," before hanging up. I asked him who that was, and I did not get any answer from him. Instead, he started looking for how to delete and block the number that had just called my phone.

I asked him, "What is wrong, Babe"?

His response was, "Don't worry, Cherie."

I asked if he knew the caller or if he was suspecting me of anything, and he did not answer me. I asked him what he was trying to do on my phone without telling me, who just called, and what was happening, but he did not answer me. I remember him and I fighting for my phone because he would not answer or tell me what was going on, and I was becoming impatient.

Eventually, I managed to get the phone from him before he deleted the number, and I told him I was calling the number to see who it was.

He told me, "No, Cherie, I have something to tell you. It's not what you think." I asked him to talk to me. He said, "I met this lady on Facebook, and she started asking me for $600 to buy food for her children and pay her phone."

I responded, "Ok. Did you give it to her?"

He said, "No, I didn't give it to her, and she got upset and said she will tell my wife."

I asked him, "So, you met a stranger on a public platform, she demanded $600, you refused, and she threatened to tell me? How did you two start the conversation?" I said. He did not answer.

"Have you slept with her?" I asked.

"No," he responded.

"Have you met her in person?" I asked.

"No," he said.

"Are you telling me the truth?" I asked.

He said, "Yes, Cherie. Please don't let anything or anyone come between us.

I know there are many people who aren't happy about our relationship and will try anything to see us fall."

I asked him if there is anything I should know, and his answer was, "Please don't listen to them."

So, I picked up the phone, called the number, and before the person on the other end could say hello, he immediately asked me to hang up and said that he wanted to talk to me. I hung up the phone to listen to what he had to say.

He said, "Please Cherie, don't be mad at me, but I felt sorry for her and gave her $400, but she was not happy because it wasn't the full amount she had asked me for... which is why she said she will tell you."

Now, I still had some hope and was fighting with my mind that what I was thinking could be a lie or was staged. He again was smart to know that my heart and passion is with women -- particularly single moms and couldn't stand to see hungry children -- so he used it as a weapon to soften me up.

I asked him where the money that he gave her came from. He wasn't working and hadn't been working for the past nine months, while I was the one paying all the bills in the house while he went to school, including his phone, credit cards, sending money to his children in Africa, to his mom in Africa, and basically sponsoring him head-to-toe. He said he took it off one of his credit cards.

I dialled the number again, feeling eager to get to the bottom of all this. The lady answered and said, "Is this sister Rebecca?"

I responded, "Yes."

She said, "Okay, please send me your WhatsApp number; I have a few messages from your husband I want to send to you." I thanked her and told her to send them to the same number she had called. (In Africa, as long as you live together, even if you're not married, they refer to you as husband and wife.)

When I got off the phone with her, Charlie said, "Cherie, you are taking this too far than it needs to be."

I told him I didn't want it to go too far, but this was his opportunity to come clean if there was anything to tell me. I told him I would love to hear it from him first rather than hearing it from my fellow lady, who ultimately knew me too well, even though I had no clue who she was.

He then admitted that he did not give her only $400, he gave her $600. He also confessed meeting up with her at the mall on the Friday I was at my brother's graduation and going to her house on Saturday, which would be the night we came home to the empty house. This man had video called me that same Friday, and we talked about each other's plan for that day, but meeting this lady was nowhere in his plans during our conversation.

In fact, I later learned that when he had video called me, he was already at the mall waiting for her. (His college was in the same mall he met her at.)

He apologized but refused to admit having sex with her despite going to her house and ultimately spending a night there. He began pacing up and down, doing what looked like messaging nonstop, all while apologizing thousands of times while maintaining his innocence. About two hours later, with failed attempts to stop her from sending the messages to me and promising her all kinds of things, she finally sent the messages to me. At that moment, I discovered I was living with a monster of a human who had paid her over $1,650 for sex in just one week.

I asked him one more time to come out clean and told him, "I have received the massages, but before I open them, I want to give you a chance to tell me from your own mouth. I'll ask you one more last time. Did you have sex or any kind of sexual contact with this woman?"

He said no.

I asked him, "Have you ever cheated on me during our relationship with anyone?"

He said, "No, I would never."

I confronted him with messages and other than an empty "sorry", everything was self-explanatory (over 100 messages). The messages were screenshots of his messages and his picture to make sure it wasn't made up. The messages ranged anywhere from meeting (he added her), making a deal, talking about how he will make her happy financially if she can be available when he wants her, positions, how it went (what he liked and didn't like), about how he hates condoms and the last two hours of him bribing her not to send them to me. The messages also revealed the reason that caused the disagreements between them, which led this woman to send me these messages.

It still makes me sick to my stomach to know this is the man I was sharing my body with and wasting all my love and energy.

After reading all this and asking him to pack up and leave immediately, I remember calling my mom shaking; I couldn't even speak. I heard my mom panicking on the phone because I couldn't finish a sentence enough to tell her what was wrong. I can vividly remember trying to say "Mom" and just not being able to. I was shaking uncontrollably. I can still see myself trying to get out of bed to get to my dresser because my heart felt like it had somehow left my body. I wanted to get to the mirror by my dresser to see if it was really me. My legs felt like jelly and were too weak to stand. I sat down about seven to ten times before I could make a full step from my bed to my dresser, and even still, I had to lean on it.

At this point, I don't know what was going on in his mind, but he wouldn't take his eyes off me as I struggled, naked, to get out of the bed and over to the dresser, while he packed up his belongings in the room. While this was going on, I had my mom on the phone, who was panicking, because at this point, I still wasn't able to pronounce the word "Mom." I would say "m" multiple times, but I couldn't explain what exactly was going on. It took a lot of effort and many tries to fully pronounce the word mom (with Mom's help of guided breathing). I eventually gained some strength to talk to her and told her what I had just read with my eyes.

After talking to Mom and feeling somewhat energized again, I responded back to the lady, and to my surprise, she offered to meet me, saying that she had more things she wanted to show me. As the very curious person that I am, I said sure. The lady sent me her address. I knew it would be a dangerous game to go by myself, so I called up one of my friends (I thought) to come with me and, sure enough, she agreed.

This "friend" and I met at a restaurant to eat first before we went, but I was too weak to even finish my juice. I waited for her to eat her food and off we went with her car and left mine behind at the restaurant. We arrived at the lady's house and she invited us in. She walked me through their entire relationship process, including some things that may be inappropriate for this book. We sat down, and two hours later a heated conversation broke among three of us. The mistress lost some of her hair, I lost my favourite watch, and the "friend", who we will refer to as Tina, lost her car keys… as well as a bit of her skin. The police came, we were all questioned, and after they made their conclusions there were no arrests or charges laid.

Fast forward, I have asked Charlie to leave and he has left. Tina, the same friend I went with to meet the mistress, comes back into play. She had been around some phone calls between Charlie and myself, so she knew we were struggling. I brought her with me to the mistress' house because she knew of our issue already. I didn't want to tell anyone else.

Tina would call to check on me almost every day after our breakup to supposedly comfort me, but while she was calling to check on me, I kept getting calls from other people telling me about seeing her with Charlie everywhere. They would tell me they saw him driving her car, but the car they were describing was the very same car Charlie had come home with after we came back from the graduation. Little did I know that Tina's enthusiasm to come with me to meet the mistress was not to help me, but to get revenge for herself.

One day his mail came, and I called him and told him to come get it at my work. Sure enough, he came with the red car that belonged to Tina and was the same car people had been describing to me. He parked so far away that you had to walk for a good three to five minutes to get where he parked. I gave him the mail and then, after he had walked back to the car and couldn't see me anymore, I decided to follow him in my car. I pulled over beside him as he was getting into the red car (Tina's), looked at him, and drove back to work.

I immediately called Tina to ask her how she could be so wicked and pretend to be a friend (by asking me how I was doing), and that I knew Charlie was staying with her -- less than a week of us separating.

She answered me, "If I wanted him, I would have had him a long time ago. I do not want him; I have five men who satisfy me anytime I want them. When they talk about men you consider your ex a man, too? Do you know how long he has been running after me like a dog? He has been after me since he added me on Facebook. You didn't want him, and I need his help, so what do you want? He doesn't live with me, but I know where he lives, who he lives with, and yes, he is using my car to go to work and to help me drop my children to day care. You didn't want him, right?"

I was shocked and hung up the phone. A few minutes later, Charlie called me to warn me to stay away from her and leave her alone.

As a child and adult, I had endured so much pain, but the pain from this experience was so sharp. This experience was by far the hardest, even as someone who endured all kinds of abuse and loses. This was not the hardest because it was the worst, but because of how much love and respect I had for this man. He was not the most handsome man I had been with, neither was he the most qualified. In fact, he was the least qualified of all -- if we were to look at class, but I had loved him purely.

I had gone into it with a "forever" mindset, and the love and respect I had for him was nothing like I had ever given before. This was a second time I had truly and willingly fell in love without any agenda or force. But this time I had fooled myself into thinking we were in this together for life. Before this experience, it would have been so hard to imagine my life without him, and that's why I was willing to drop on to my knees to beg for forgiveness, even when I believed I wasn't wrong -- but not this time.

Sistergirl, in this incident alone, I had three people (and more who came after) who hurt me so badly that I needed a release to set me free. I needed to set Rebecca free by forgiving Charlie, the mistress, and the so-called friend Tina. Boy oh boy, was it hard. I had to release them for myself so I could pick up my pieces one-by-one again and make myself a whole again. It was not easy, and it surely took a lot of intention, self-reflection, and a whole lot of help from close family, friends, and co-workers.

During my healing process I reached out to Charlie to ask him what I did wrong or what was missing from me to the point he felt he needed to pay for sex, while he got it from me whenever he wanted (if not at work, of course). His response was, "I don't know. I really don't know what came over me." On the same call, Charlie went on to tell me, "Rebecca, I loved you so much and even left my wife for you. I know I lied to you that we were separated when I met you, and lied to you about all the things she did, but I actually only left her when I met you because I wanted to be with you."

Honey, this healing journey wasn't a joke. I had to take two weeks off work to recover, and I had to send my children away because I was too weak to even care for them or make them a meal. All I did was sleep and order takeout… and sometimes even forgot to eat it. I had to avoid people because I would start sobbing just looking into someone's eyes.

No matter how much I showered or what kind of feminine washing products I used, the feeling of cleanliness felt far from reach. I slept a lot to escape my reality and had illusions that perhaps, just maybe, when I woke up it would just be a nightmare; but it was my reality. I wept many tears for many days and nights.

During this time, with the help of a few friends in business who encouraged me, I mastered the courage to travel to Dallas, Texas. I had already purchased my ticket prior for a business event. While there, I was cheered and comforted by a few of my friends and one of Charlie's close friends, who later became like a sister to me.

This woman nurtured me during this time, and I am forever thankful to her! While we are on this note; I would be very naïve if I didn't acknowledge my three amazing co-workers. They became my counsellors, my brothers, spoke life into me inside and outside of work, and I am grateful for them. Thank you, Mike, Nickman, and Mr. T!

During one of my reflection moments, I remembered a story Charlie had told me about how he hated and resented his father and stepmom for a long time before warming up to her and forgiving his father. As per Charlie, his father had left Charlie's mother pregnant with no food and went to a business trip only to settle there with another woman without even informing her, which led to his mother becoming depressed and eventually miscarrying.

I also remembered a conversation I had with his mom when I had called her to let her know what had happened between us, and her response to me was, "If every man who cheats on you, you run away -- how many husbands will people count for you?"

I was speechless and shocked by her response and her entire reaction, but I had to keep calm and respect her as an elder.

This incident, along with the way my family treated me, especially during my pregnancy, made me realize that people are hurting from all corners of life. And, while we want to love them and support them, it is not our job to stop them from hurting as that is an internal job -- along with professional help. We can listen and love them from distance, but we cannot afford or allow ourselves to continue being their victims by ignoring red flags or continuously putting them before us.

We can avoid being victims by setting boundaries of what we allow and won't allow, and by setting non-negotiable standards of how we want to be treated. Had I acted on the red flags, dug deeper into the family history or paid attention to our conversations, and questioned where he was going while I was at work, then I may have avoided some of the outcome that left me in bed for two weeks. His actions hurt not only me, but they wounded my children as well (who adored and loved him to pieces). I will not hesitate to drop anybody like a hot potato who tries to cross my non-negotiable boundaries or to make me a victim of their undealt with problems -- family or not.

As for Charlie and his ladies, I have forgiven them and respond to his texts when he texts, but loving him from a distance is the best I can do for the both of us since our values don't align.

Please understand that playing victim does not help anybody. It hurts you and the other people who eventually become your victims as well. I would also like to add that we almost always have a part in whatever happens to us as adults by allowing people to continuously press and control our lives because we put those buttons there. I don't say this for you to beat yourself up; I say this so you can re-evaluate and see what you are allowing someone else to do to you. What are you giving them control over? You may have been abused as a young girl like myself and unfortunately, while that may live with you for the rest of your life, I urge you to think of what you can do to avoid this from happening to your children or any other child.

You may be being physically abused by your partner or parents or whoever. They may be abusing you emotionally, financially, or in other forms, but you continue to make the choice to stay because of the kids or what people will say. This is bull; it's an excuse. It is a well-planned giant lie you are telling yourself. You are in captivity, and you must do everything possible to break the chains so you can free yourself and your children. You are your own and children's rescuer, and until you desire to be free and seek help, no one can help you. I know it may seem impossible to break away from whatever is holding you back, but I urge for you to do it faster, so that you can start your healing journey sooner.

I had to find a way to run away from home at sixteen years old, seven months pregnant, and just after two months in a foreign country with no language, not even one single friend to lean on or talk to, no pennies in my pocket, not allowed to communicate with the father of my child and in winter season. In any unhealthy situation, any time and any day is a perfect time to break free!

In my case with Charlie, who broke me to pieces, I saw many red flags; but I fell for what I wanted it to be and kept holding onto empty hopes. I ignored what it was.

I am not advocating for a separation or breakup when there is cheating involved as everybody's stand on this is different, and that's your choice to make. For me, I knew I didn't want to be with someone I couldn't trust. After all, where there is a will there's a way, and he would most likely still find another way even if you had his phone 24/7.

I only used my experience of my most recent task of forgiving, but please know when to put your foot down and say enough is enough. Set boundaries, look for repetitive behaviours, and lies. Know your worth and if need be – love them from a distance. While I loved and adored Charlie with everything in my veins and bones, even as I told him to pack up and get lost, I was willing to let him go in the blink of an eye and love him from a distance as a person.

He had crossed my boundaries and his actions did not align with the values and morals I want to teach my children. Not only did his actions not align with my moral values, I had been abused as a little girl, and here I was raising a young, beautiful girl (twelve years old at the time) who adored him. If he was not content with my sacrifices (of me working day and night to support us while he is in school to better himself) so much so as to pay for sex using my hard-earned cash -- how was I supposed to be sure he wasn't going to turn to my daughter? He had taken all my love and honour I had for him and discarded it across the ocean. He had crossed my non-negotiable line, and it was time for me to wake up, put my foot down, and toss his ass out of my life.

REFLECTION

Think of who you must release immediately. Someone you need to let go faster so you can start healing sooner. Then think of what your non-negotiable line is. The boundaries you are not willing to let anyone cross. Lastly, who are you allowing to cross them now, and what will you do about it? Make a list if it helps.

You can do the same with habits or patterns you find yourself repeating.

BONUS SECRET

Betty Ogiel

Do you sometimes feel like life is against you, no matter how much you try? I am honoured to introduce to you a dear friend of mine who not only has proven time and time again that no matter what the odds against you may be, if you don't give up you shall overcome! You may be born with a "shovel" in your mouth instead of a gold or silver spoon, but with hard work and determination you can turn that shovel into a golden spoon! Betty's story: a brain injury survivor who jumped from a wheelchair to high heels shares her story of a life against all odds!

Betty Ogiel is the founder of the Betty Ogiel Foundation, an author of the award-winning book *Against All Odds*: Memoirs of Resilience, Determination and Luck Amidst Hardship for an African Girl Child in Her Passionate Pursuit for Education. Ogiel is also an inspirational speaker whose mission is to inspire hope and transform lives. She is also a certified independence coach with the John Maxwell Team and a Human Resource Excellence Award as well as Peacemaker Award recipient.

IN HER WORDS

I am among those people born without a silver spoon in their mouth but with a shovel in her hands instead. My early life was characterized by lack in every aspect. From the onset of my life, there were early signs that the journey ahead of me would be a troubled one.

I was orphaned at early age when I lost my father Samson Icaarat, who was a rising leader in Teso. He had already risen to the rank of a sub-parish chief. Our humble family of nine that lived happily together in a mud and wattle grass thatched hut was seen as a model. But there is a way that poverty tends to bring out the worst in human beings. My father's progress drew envy in the community.

One day my father stopped at a corner restaurant for a quick meal. Little did he know the food had been laced with poison. Dad died on his way back home, leaving behind seven children with a young wife who could not fend for her children single-handedly. I was only three years old when this unfortunate incident occurred.

The clan members held the future of my siblings and I in their hands. I was "given" to Nicholas, a paternal uncle and last-born brother of my father, to be raised in his home. Uncle Nicholas was about to complete his teacher training course and was set to start teaching at Kalas Girls' Primary School in Amudat district in Karamoja region. In the Iteso culture, when a father prematurely dies, the brother of the deceased inherits the widow. The idea here is to create social harmony as most of the women then did not have an independent income.

Still a bachelor, Uncle, with ideas of a bright life ahead, probably did not want to start out with a widow and her seven children. A compromise was finally reached. Nicholas would take and raise young Betty. The rest of the children were removed from the care of my mother too and split among relatives.

Nicholas secured a teaching job in Amudat, one of Uganda's poorest district in Karamoja. Karamoja is a pastoral community where natives rely primarily on cattle and engage in sparse agriculture. The land is dry, bushy and thorny, only experiencing scattered rainfall. Education, until of late, was never a priority -- more so for girls. To this day, many Karimojong believe all the cows in the world belong to them. A proud warrior tribe, like their sister tribe the Masai, cattle rustling is a pastime.

At the age of six, Uncle Nicholas took me to Amudat to raise and educate me, and got me enrolled at Kalas Girls Primary School. But a lack of school fees was a problem right from the beginning, and I was only able to complete primary education through a bursary from the Christian Children's Fund, by virtue of Nicholas being a teacher at the school.

Uncle Nicholas did not have children of his own at the time. I saw him struggle through two failed relations until he settled on one. A foster mother who, I would say, was sent from hell to torment me. With the new foster mother in the home, I instantaneously became an unpaid housemaid. I do not recall playing as a child. My daily routine in Amudat began at 6:00 a.m. My life revolved around home, school, and doing all household chores — cooking, washing, and fetching water five kilometres away from home in the hot and scorching sun of Karamoja. If I ever came short of my foster mother's expectations, I would earn myself a thorough beating from her. I developed multiple wounds and scars. In one such flogging, Uncle Nicholas accidently came home. The two ended up quarrelling and fighting. Since I was the cause, the flogging became even more severe in the absence of Uncle Nicholas.

Finally, he took me to a missionary boarding school so my foster mother would not torture me anymore. Here, I constantly suffered from scabies and jiggers. I remember the unbearable suffering I went through those days under the scourge of scabies. It was an epidemic that affected many of us, and it was contagious and no one in school wore shoes. There was no adequate treatment for it. A person infested with scabies would really suffer physical and emotional trauma, not to mention the jesting that you would receive from other children. These two scourges really made it difficult for us.

One constant reminder of my hardship was that I owned one navy blue dress, which I wore every day. I wore my favourite and only dress for years before my uncle bought me another one, and only after he had been put on the spot by the neighbours in Amudat. The dress got torn, and in a spur of creativity, I cut it up, and it effectively became a skirt. Remember, I was still under ten years old, so you can be sure that this child was already taking care of herself.

Despite all these hardships, God had given me a gift: I had a good mind. This enabled me to make easy progress in school. While in primary six, a teacher noticed my athleticism. Through their encouragement, I took up the sport and represented my school at the Annual District Athletics competition in Moroto district in 1990. I was the youngest. I wore a dress, the same dress that I had worn for as long as I could remember. One dress worn daily for years. That was my athletics costume that day as well.

Just before I completed my primary education, our school was raided by Karamojong warriors. Together with my fellow pupils and villagers, we ran for dear life and ended up in Natemeri in Northern Kenya. The warriors had raided the school for food supplies. The attack left one child dead.

After successfully sitting my Primary Living Exams, I had a hunger to continue my education. I waited for Uncle Nicholas to take me to the nearby Secondary, but though he was an educated man, he saw no need to help me go beyond Primary level of education. He had done his part and probably expected a suitor to come along. Most girls afflicted with poverty do not go far in school and parents just marry them off, or some get pregnant and start raising children. My fate seemed sealed. Each time I would plead to go back to school, the answer was instant and harsh. No money! When Uncle Nicholas failed to raise school fees for my secondary education and all seemed lost, I cried for days until he succumbed to pressure from neighbours to do something about it. I had become so attached to education and learning that I could not, for a minute, fathom a life without school. I had seen my mom left behind by her husband, who was a sub-parish chief struggling to make a living. In fact, I know that she would go for months on end before seeing a single coin.

But I had also another gift: determination. Despite all the beatings I had received from my foster mother, my spirit had never been suppressed. Where others would have given in, each day, I would wail loudly that I wanted to go back to school.

My biggest driving force was the need to complete my higher education so I could lead a better life than what my dear mom lived. Second, I really desired to help my mother and siblings.

Following the neighbours' intervention, Uncle Nicholas enrolled me at Arengesiep Senior Secondary School in present day Nabilatuk district. Even then he could not afford the full fees of Uganda shillings 24,000 ($6.4). Nevertheless, he took me to school three weeks to the end of the first term and paid only a half of the fees. This school was so remote that it did not have the features of a standard school, you could not differentiate a teacher from students, and there were also Karimojong warriors in this school. School was not easy. To get back home during the holidays, I often had to hitchhike rides (sometimes on tractors) as there was no one to pick me up. The roads were always dangerous, and once I survived an ambush from cattle rustlers.

When I found that it was the athletics season at Arengesiep, I immersed myself in running and excelled. I was selected to represent the school at the district competition and single-handedly elevated the school's sporting standing by winning the one, two, four, and eight hundred-meter races. I had had no formal coaching.

When I returned home in Amudat for the school holiday, I was shocked to find that Uncle had sought a transfer back to Teso after separating from his wife and had abandoned me in Karamoja. He had left the house keys with the neighbours since he knew I would come for the school holiday.

It dawned on me that the only family member I loved and knew had abandoned me. I was alone and frightened.

It was bad enough to be separated from my mother. It was enough to be mistreated by my foster mother. It was enough to live in poverty. It was enough to barely make it to secondary school. Until now, I had handled all those odds blow-by-blow, and I was at par with them. This was unbelievable as it was unexpected.

I had a very strong urge to forge on in my life. So, I took stock of my situation. I looked around the house and I found that there was a good stock of maize grain. I knew what I needed to do; I would brew malwa (local alcoholic beverage). Uncle's wife had taught me all there was to know about this traditional alcoholic beverage, from brewing to selling, and I knew I could pull it off.

I had a dream which needed to be funded for me to achieve it. I made decision to work and not pity myself; God had blessed me with hardworking hands. So, to raise fees for the next term, I brewed and sold malwa every day of the holiday break. I kept all the money that I made, except what I would use daily to buy food. I could have bought shoes and meat, things that I craved, but I did not. Of course, I bought myself some dresses which, to me, was a great achievement.

I noticed that a friend's mother was also a good traditional brewer who smuggled waragi (local potent gin) to the lucrative market in neighbouring

Kenya. I talked her into letting me join the smuggling excursions into Kenya.

But our luck ran out when on the second smuggling trip we were intercepted by Kenyan police. Our waragi had given us away as it had a very strong and distinct smell. We were saved by one considerate police officer, who said, "Leave the old woman and her daughter alone. They are merely trying to eke out a living in these tumultuous times we live in." And that is how we escaped being prosecuted and jailed in Kenya. Had we been arrested, I do not know what would have happened to us.

My enterprise was profitable enough to take care of my school needs to such an extent that I paid all my full year fees balances at Arengesiep. After realizing that I had a bit of money, I took a bold step and sought admission at the school of my dreams -- Kangole Girls Senior Secondary School in Moroto.

I joined in the first term of Senior Two in 1993, and I promised the school administration the school dues would be paid later. That was the last time I would see Amudat, a place that shaped me against all the odds of my life. I decided I would not go back. I closed the malwa brewing business.

One evening, a missions organization that works among students, Scripture Union, came calling. Feeling down and hopeless, I attended the Youth Alive session and listened attentively. The preacher seemed to speak to me directly. The message was that God knew my school fees situation and that He would take care of me.

Indeed, a few nights later while walking back to my dormitory, after night preps, a snake bit me. I was rushed to the nearby dispensary run by Catholic nuns where I was treated using the traditional Blackstone method, as I could not raise the fees for contemporary medicine. The stone is used to suck out the poison.

Sister Susan Anyango, a Catholic nun from the Society of Sacred Heart Community, took pity on me and inquired about my troubled life. She noticed that I was completely on my own with no visitor or caretaker, let alone a relative beside me. She was a God-sent angel, who promised to have me enrolled in the needy students' scheme. You cannot quantify my joy when I heard this. To think this breakthrough was brought about by a snakebite is mind-boggling. My school fees' challenges became a thing of the past.

Had I not been incapacitated by that snake bite, chances are my predicament would not have come to the attention of the nuns. I got into the needy students' scheme and my secondary school fees were paid. I completed my Ordinary level education and passed.

I knew that the only way to come out of poverty was through school, but that education was not necessarily the silver bullet against poverty. So, during all holidays, I worked as a casual labourer picking cotton at the Serere Agricultural Research Institute farms. After picking cotton at the farm, I heard that Uganda the police was recruiting and applied. When the officer saw my grades, he pointed out that I had performed well and then proceeded to ask, "Why give up on school?" I felt this was another angel pointing me to the right direction. But then where would I get school fees?

My relatives were financially hard up. Sister Anyango was my only hope. I got in touch with her and learned that she had just gotten posted to St. Charles Lwanga Girls Training Center-Kalungu in Masaka district. She invited me to Masaka, where she was stationed at a Sacred Heart Nuns convent. She wanted me to continue with my studies under the nuns' care.

With my savings, I paid my fees for the first term at St. Charles Lwanga Girls Training Centre. It was another opportunity to feel proud of myself for catering to all my expenses at school.

Sister Anyango got me registered on the list of needy students, and once again the convent's solidarity fund paid my fees. I took my studies seriously, knowing this was my only passport out of poverty. My mother had died after a hard life without a regular income. All my six siblings had dropped out of school. I was the last hope. I dreamed of a better life, not only for me, but the rest of my family. I completed my Advanced level education and scored fifteen points, just one point less for a government university scholarship.

I was admitted to Makerere University, though on a private scheme, I narrowly missed the government scholarship. A benefactor paid for my first semester's tuition and once again I struggled to raise the fees for the subsequent semester. My old problem of fees was back to torment me again. Sister Anyango could no longer support me on her own. After raising some money for tuition, I also had to secure accommodation. Luckily, I found a Christian couple who boarded students. But that situation did not work out well due to lack of space. So, I decided to move out and secure a sleeping place at the university sports field. Several students had already been murdered in the vicinity. But I had no alternative as I could not afford hostel accommodation. I had come too far with my struggles to give up at the last huddle.

The university's Dean of Students got wind of a girl sleeping down at the university sports ground. What if that girl was raped and possibly murdered? The dean ordered me out immediately. *Where else now to get accommodation? But hadn't the Scripture Union preacher said God knew my situation?* True. A friend advised me to talk to the deputy vice chancellor.

Professor Justin Epelu-Opio, was also from Teso. He too had come up the hard way. He was already helping with fees of many struggling students. *Would he help me out?* I wondered. Without hesitation, I reached out and poured out my heart to the professor. Touched by my predicament, he sympathized with me and offered to pay my fees until I graduated. What a huge relief. I thanked God for another angel in my life.

But still, I could not raise accommodation fees and was forced to convert the makeshift sports pavilion into my hostel once again. I lived there throughout the college days.

I put all my energies into my studies and excelled. I graduated with an upper second-class degree in social sciences, narrowly missing a first-class degree, and became the first person in my clan to attain a university degree.

My first job was as a research fellow at Makerere's Institute of Social Research. Later, I was recruited by the International Audit firm, where my performance was impeccable. This opened doors for me to join a multinational oil company as a human resource officer. I then pursued a post graduate diploma in human resource at Uganda Management Institute. My classmates elected me president.

Success comes at a cost. While I was successful, I had the burden of the rest of my family that looked up to me. This is common in Africa for the few who are successful, especially from hard-up families. They are expected to shoulder the rest.

One day after taking care of some hectic work and family matters, I was driving from my ancestral home in Ongongoja, Katakwi, Eastern Uganda, heading to Kampala (capital city of Uganda) when I lost control of the vehicle which veered off the road and hit a tree. All five of us in the vehicle (my 4-year-old son, a sister, myself, and two cousin sisters) survived, although I was the most affected.

To make matters worse, those who came to rescue us mercilessly helped themselves to the property of accident victims. I laid on the road unconscious until an angel came through. A good samaritan took us to a nearby hospital in Kampala approximately 200k from the accident scene.

My speech was virtually wiped out due to brain injuries. Part of my body was paralyzed. The once breezing runner could neither talk nor walk. It seemed like my fate had been finally sealed. But the girl who had come that far was not about to give up. God was not done with me yet. I fought back and through effort, persistence, and eternal optimism, I gradually recovered much of my speech back, and I also started to walk again.

I have come from far, and seen almost everything, yes everything. I have never lost the spark of life, nor faith in a good God. What reason do you have to lose hope and give up on your dream? It takes determination, hard work, resilience, and passion to achieve your dream; there is no shortcut. I have achieved a lot in life because of this. I am an inspirational speaker whose mission is to inspire hope and transform lives. I am an author and an award-winning human resource manager. I am a recipient of several awards; in 2016 and 2017, I received the Human Resource Excellence Award consecutively in the category of Employee Engagement awarded by the Human Resource Manager's Association of Uganda. In September 2017, I received the Peacemaker Award from the Global Prosperity and Peace Initiative in addition to several best employee awards in my name. I am also a certified independent coach, speaker, and trainer with the John Maxwell Team. I train and coach individuals and corporate companies using the John Maxwell Leadership resources.

I host the monthly inspirational Against All Odds Talks in Kampala, organized by the Betty Ogiel foundation. This is a foundation that I founded to transform lives, especially of the destitute girl child from Karamoja. The talks are designed for sharing knowledge and inspirational ideas through real-life stories. Proceeds from the talks go to the foundation to educate needy children. Currently, there are five students receiving full academic scholarships. My dream for this foundation is to have an inspirational centre where we can train and empower people to believe in themselves and achieve their full potential in life.

After failed relationships, I am married to Rubanga Julius Abunga and we have been blessed with three sons.

My goodness, what a life of resilience, determination, and luck amidst hardship for an African girl child in her passionate pursuit for education.

If you would like to connect with Betty or to learn more about her story, please purchase her book by visiting her website at www.againstallodds.life or by using the search term "against all odds" on Amazon. You can also email her at bettyogielfoundation@gmail.com.

5

Secret Five
Becoming Confident in Your Decision-Making and Owning it

One of the worst things you can do for yourself is to try to be somebody you're not to please others. This pleasing business puts stress and pressure on you. It limits you and the amazing things you can discover about yourself.

My dear fellow single mama, you may wish to volunteer at your child's school, but single mom's demands and the corporate world get in the way. I want to tell you that it is perfectly okay for you to not be on every single school trip, and please never, ever beat yourself up for it. Other parents may look like they have it all together while you are running around in your PJs with unbrushed hair in a ponytail or afro (if you are a hot chocolate like me), but it is okay. Your child may throw a temper at the park because they are mad at you and miss their daddy; hold your child and talk to them -- who cares what those other moms think of you? You may be the only one sitting there with kids at your family reunion, but just enjoy the meal and the family. Your time to have a partner is coming if that's your desire. You may feel bad for the kids and feel the need to fill in for daddy, but please do not -- you are a mummy. You are doing your best and that is enough.

This past Father's Day (2020), I posted a note celebrating myself for Father's Day, and I remember a few comments from people who don't believe in this. I don't try to be a father and clearly as you may already guessed, I damn love me as a woman and wouldn't for a second want to be or take a man's place. Unfortunately, as single mothers, we are forced to fill in for both roles that were designed for two parents. After all, we don't celebrate only those who planted or donated sperm; we celebrate spiritual fathers and adoptive fathers because they are the ones RAISING the child (doing the biological father's job). However, if the father is in your child's life and is willingly doing his part, please honour him despite your relationship differences.

Your friends are out having a blast at a friend's party but you can't go because you don't have a babysitter and this reminds you of that b*****d who got you pregnant and left you to you to do the raising part alone; enjoy your child(ren). I promise they won't always be that little and require a sitter.

You have a special date, but you are forced to cancel it because your babysitter cancelled on you last minute. What if that was a sign that it wouldn't have been worth it anyway?

You are exhausted from work but have to go pick up kids from the babysitter, start cooking, and then prepare them for bed or run them to their soccer practice -- it's all right, mama. It's temporary.

By now, I think I have mentioned something that resonates with how you felt at some point or may feel along your single parenting journey, but my prayer is that you will be comforted with knowing that your children will not always be that small. I hope you will condition your mind to enjoy whatever is happening regardless of how uncomfortable it may be. It is easy to curse the dad, but honestly, if I have my children, even as hard as it is doing everything on my own, it is his loss. Give yourself permission to be upset, to be tired, or to look a little crazy. Do what you feel is best without compromising yourself in the name of trying to compete or compare yourself to anyone or to look like other moms.

Another big issue we single parents face is we sometimes get in the way of our authenticity is decision-making. There are stigmas and stereotypes regarding single parenting. At times, it honestly feels as though everyone has something to say about what we should or should not do.

I used to think I experienced this so much because I had gotten pregnant at a very young age (made a wrong choice already) and this may have led people to believe I wasn't capable of making good decisions. But as I grew older and started befriending other single mamas who had experienced the same thing, even though they were married and mature when they had their babies, I realized it wasn't just me. This is what society has been led to believe about single moms.

I remember I once texted a good friend of mine to ask his opinion on whether I should buy a house or pay off all my debt first, and his answer blew me away.

He said, "Do you want me to give you an honest answer?"

I said, "Yes, please!"

Then he said, "I think you should pay off all your debt first because as much as it is very hard to date single mom, especially in your case with three children, if you have all your sh*t together, he can close his eyes and take on the responsibility."

Now, I know my friend meant well and the advice about paying off all debt was incredibly good advice, but his reasoning behind the idea felt very wrong. The way he phrased it seemed like anybody who gets in a relationship with me would be doing me a big favour. Without knowing, he made me feel like I am not dateable unless I was a certain way or had a certain level of achievement. Thank goodness I know my worth and what I bring to the table. But hearing this from a good friend could really have a big impact on how we look at ourselves, which is why I started with knowing your self-worth.

I know that people can take away monetary possessions or abuse my kindness, but no one can take away my determination, my resiliency, my tenacity, and there is definitely no one on this earth who can convince me I ain't smoking hot! It took me an awfully long time to find a way around this struggle in order to reclaim my decision-making powers, as well as knowing my worth. It took me an incredible amount of tries, disappointments, doubts, and even cost me a few friends, who I do not miss at all.

It wasn't easy because, just like everyone, I had people who I admired (especially those who spoke to my heart), those who had what I desired, the family who I adored, and friends. You probably already know this, and I can bet you have said it at least ten times in your life, but we often say things like, "I want to be like_." But the truth is we only like what we see; we don't know what goes on behind closed curtains. We don't know what they went through to get to the point we like them at. They may have had to put in a few tears into their marriage, a few sleepless nights, and miss a few parties to work on their dream. They may have slept in their car for three years before speaking on stage to thousands of people. They may have been raped by family members and writing was their way of coping with that trauma, which eventually became the New York Times Best Seller. Do you really want to be like them? Are you willing to do those things that got them there? Are you mentally ready? They probably had to take time to heal from their past trauma first. Have you taken this step?

I have people that I love and admire very much such as Lisa Nichols, my parents, and friends. I also admire people who have achieved some amazing success like John C. Maxwell, Iyanla Vanzant, Dani Johnson, and the late Dr. Myles Munroe; however, it is very important we understand the difference between wanting to "be like them" and "modelling" the work we see and appreciate. There is no copy and paste in this life.

What I am trying to say is -- true happiness means picking and choosing what will work for you, and make sure your piece of pie is the first and biggest part. This means you do not copy and paste. Trying to copy and paste another person's life is just a wish and the quickest way to lower self-esteem. Like I explained earlier, you and I both know there is only one of us, we will never be another person. You may have success that looks like Oprah Winfrey, but you will never be her. You may achieve all the success in the world, but still feel lost and unsatisfied because you have lost yourself in the effort of trying to become another person you will never be. So, starting today, find yourself first and fall madly in love with you!

Like I mentioned previously, this had been a struggle for me for many years, but particularly in my early years of parenting. I struggled to keep up with other moms that were in the same shelter I was in. I thought it was bad enough that I was so in love with my baby, but always felt less of a mom and felt embarrassed to talk to or about my baby whenever I was around other moms; however, the struggle got even more serious when I moved out.

After moving out of the shelter, I rented a room in a couple's home who had young children. The wife was very good with her kids, had a routine going, she sang to them, read to them, and just seemed like she had everything together, while even talking to my child around people was a struggle. Many people did not know, but I was super embarrassed and did not enjoy talking about being a mom nor talking to my baby around people. I would immediately brush it off and try to drive the conversation somewhere else whenever they complimented me or my baby.

My family and I had hidden my pregnancy and baby from people for so long, which included our extended family in Africa, that I didn't enjoy acknowledging this new chapter of my life publicly. I cut connections with all my childhood classmates and friends out of shame. This was due to my pregnancy experiences (all the shaming comments I'd heard that I still held on to and had carried it into my parenting unconsciously). Since I felt so shameful, I didn't feel worthy to be myself. So I started trying everything my landlady did. I bought the same books she read, looked up the songs she sang, and it became exhausting; I started feeling sort of stupid, and I felt like I was not a good mom despite other people complementing me on how great I was doing. I wished to be my authentic self in my parenting and to not try to be like others or compare myself to everyone around me (who seemed to do better in my eyes). It could have saved me a lot of heartache and could have helped me enjoy my baby earlier.

Trying to be just like her by copying and pasting what she did rather than asking myself why I felt that way, and perhaps asking her for help or seeking counselling, left me bowing down to what I had felt during those times in my early years – feeling unwanted and unworthy of anyone's love.

As the years went by, I eventually dealt with my insecurities, had more babies, and enjoyed being a mama! Being a mama is my hardest job because it's constant, but it is by far my most favourite of all the jobs I have done or ever will do. I had to deal with myself first. I thought, *Why did I feel embarrassed about my precious baby who meant the world to me?*

Although I consider myself one of the best mommas out there, I still am not like my former landlady and definitely don't want to be. I am the best mummy for my babies, just like she was for hers, and that's the most beautiful thing about authenticity. You are the best mama for your baby/babies!

She was a stay-at-home mom and her husband worked from home, while I am a single mom juggling two jobs and chasing my dreams. So, I would be doing myself a disservice by comparing my parenting skills to hers or anybody else's. Her parenting skills aren't better than mine, but having more time and a fourth arm goes a long way. You can only be best for people you need to be there for and that's yourself and your children.

Again, I want to strongly emphasize the importance of owning your decisions and taking full responsibility of any consequences/outcomes that come along. As single parents, we do not have that second opinion from a partner like a two-parent home. Nothing is wrong with seeking a second opinion, but from my experience, I know it can get a bit muddy in the sense that once you allow people into your business, some people feel you must do what they say. They forget you are only asking for their opinion, not a decision. Another thing I found is once it involves them, you subconsciously feel the urge to update them, which can leave you feeling exhausted. This is how I interpret it to feel, unlike brainstorming with your partner who you most likely share the interest in the matter and will bear the outcome together.

I remember a time when I consulted someone so dear to me about their take on a relationship I was contemplating going into. This particular relationship was with an ex of mine. We had ended it with when I went back to school because he felt I didn't have time for him, and it had become too exhausting juggling between keeping him happy, school, and kids.

I was reconsidering him because we had not had any big arguments nor any unusual misunderstandings before I went to school, which put a strain on our relationship. We had also been friends for about eight years and had admired each other, so it was super important to us to give it another try.

Fast forward, we went back into a relationship and less than a year later he started showing signs of mental illness, which quickly became worse. I begged him to get help, which he would agree to go one minute and refuse the next. I took days off work to go support him on his appointments only for him to cancel them saying that he was not sick. He outright refused help and dismissed my plea for him to get help, even after the doctor's recommendations. He said he wasn't sick and had zero interest in seeing a psychiatrist. It got to the point where it became a dangerous situation for me and the kids, so I decided to end it. He did not want help and I had children to protect. Of course, I was incredibly sad. Again, he wasn't a bad person; it was an illness, but my children needed me to protect them. I worried about him; the guilt tore me apart as I let him go because I felt I was supposed to help him.

This was another wound that needed to heal. So, I vented to few trusted people and got some counselling through my work. While talking to someone, I remember a person, who I cherish, telling me, "You do realize that decisions you make don't only hurt you but hurts the people who care about you as well." I was shocked, especially at the timing, but I had to own it because I am the one who had invited her into my mess. And as much as she was hurting for me, I am the only person who knows my why and what I truly felt. I totally agree that people who love and care about our happiness do feel pain, to some degree, when we are hurt, but don't buy into the pressure of doing what someone else wants because they care about you. I will give you a few simple steps you can take when asking for someone's input without compromising your decision-making powers.

Think of all the people who love and care about you. Now think of all their opinions, which often feels like it's the right thing to do. Always remember: when someone gives you advice or their opinion, it's based on what *they* would do -- not what you would do. Now can you imagine if you must make your decisions based on your family member's opinions? All your siblings, your closest cousins, different books, and videos you watch that often contradict each other? How about your besties? Are their likes your likes? Do those people run their every decision by you? If not, do you think they never make decisions in their lives? Is your past the same as theirs? Our experiences are huge factors in our decisions. Do you desire the same lifestyle? Are your responsibilities the same as theirs? Please do not get me wrong. It is a very good idea to get advice from family and friends you trust. It is also good to learn from influencers who have what you desire by reading books on parenting or whatever you want to learn. But your skin MUST be in the game; in fact, it should be at the centre of the game. Take time to break things down for YOU and be as honest as you can about it. Ask yourself if it is really what you desire, if that's what you want, or if it is what will make your family, community, and friends happy. Really ask yourself if this decision is yours or theirs.

There are no journeys without roadblocks, and you must be ready and willing to continue pressing on when barriers come your way; you must be ready and willing to jump those mountains. You must be 110 percent prepared to bear any consequences without blaming, pointing the finger at anyone, or regretting any outcome if things don't go as planned.

People's opinions and advice meant the world to me in my earlier adulthood. I made so many decisions that were not mine, which I greatly regretted. I was in total misery. I made decisions for my family, friends, and even for my community – all for what was right in their eyes. I didn't want to appear as if I didn't value their advice. I just wanted to be accepted but for who I was not. I did this for far too long before I started living and putting myself first.

It was so bad that I even went into relationships, including one marriage to a total stranger in another country, because a person I trusted, cherished, and considered my best friend had recommended him. She told me all juicy things about him. She was much older than I, which I guess proved to be wiser in my books. We always talked about life and she knew my needs, so I assumed she had my best interest at heart when she recommended him. She told me why he was the best choice for me and that he was "like a brother to her and would not hesitate to marry him if he wasn't her brother." After the tables turned and the truth came out, I discovered they used to date and things didn't work out. I also learned he had a family I never knew about. My so-called best friend vanished after this.

I was stuck with a marriage certificate and no husband (after exactly thirty days of marriage), along with an empty bank account, shame, and resentment. The shame and resentment I felt was so deep that I moved away shortly after. I didn't think I could control my anger if I ever saw this woman again. I left my job, my home, and family because of the shameful thoughts like, *What will people say? Can I handle meeting this woman in the store or in someone's house, look into her eyes, and not cause a scene?*

I hated and resented this woman. I regretted meeting her and trusting her. I felt stupid. I became jobless and depressed. I started avoiding people and stopped communicating altogether with people in that community because I didn't want to be asked about him or what happened. I left my three-bedroom home, with no one chasing me out, and took refuge in my spiritual sister's three-bedroom home with my three children, her two children, and her husband eight hours away on St. Joseph Island.

My children and I were the only black family on this island, which came with isolation and a cultural void for me.

St. Joseph Island is in the northwestern part of Lake Huron with population approximately 1,240 residents, 30 kilometres (19 mi) in length, 20 kilometres (12 mi) in width at its widest point, and 365 km2 (141 sq. mi) in area.

Now, I had a tremendous amount of support from my spiritual family, and my children's school was phenomenal and they loved it, but the communication and hobbies were so different for me as I am generally not an outdoor person and hate the cold to the core. It was very hard to make friends, and I think it could have been because the island is so small and everyone knows everybody else; so, there is that outsider feeling where you're trying to break in. During this time, I experienced so much love, learned a lot about many things, crafted few ideas down of which direction I wanted my life to go.

Owning your decisions occurs when you make your choices based on your truth and your instinct; it is complete when you are in agreement and at peace with your decision.

Immediately after this relationship ended, between July and September, while I waited for my kids to complete that school year so we could move to St. Joseph Island, one of my other good friends at the time introduced me to this young, gentle Indian guy. This guy was a fortune-teller who was going to tell me "what's wrong and bring my husband back."

I tell you, desperate ain't sexy at all, Sistergirl, and it definitely doesn't help you reason well. I knew I didn't want him back, but I was so desperate for answers. I wanted to speak to him face to face so I could understand why he would feel the need to betray me like he did. We hadn't ever had an argument except when I found out about his actual age just two days after our wedding, which was more than ten years difference from what he had originally told me.

I was so desperate to know why I couldn't have the happy family I longed for. I felt desperate and angry. I was so worried about what everyone would think or say. I was so desperate for answers from the wrong medium. As a believer, the only mediator I should have looked to for answers should have been Christ, who God himself sent as a medium between him and his people (us). I was so desperate that I used my $10,000 line of credit and drove over two hours each weekend or twice a weekend instead of spending that time with my children. It's also evident that I felt disoriented for a very long time, felt like I had failed my children, and I vowed to put myself first for my own sake. I vowed to create happiness for myself instead of looking for it where it isn't, whether it be in people or things.

Throughout my life, I have learned that not owning your decisions, because you are trying to please others, and saying no to yourself are the worst mistakes you can ever make. When you make and base your decisions on what others want, in order to please someone else or are worried about what they will think if you don't do what they say, you start singing, "I wish I didn't listen." You start blaming others and avoid taking accountability for your actions. People who love you will empathize with you, they will be hurting for you, but the truth of the matter is that they will never feel what you feel no matter how much they love you. Not even your mama who birthed you or your children you birthed can feel your pain. Let your decision be SOLELY yours and not your mother's, sister's, brother's, mentor's, neighbour's, or best friend's.

Take accountability and admit the mistakes you have contributed to, for whatever is hindering you, and then mend and move on. Do not beat yourself up for it. Learn from it. Release all guilt and shame and step out in full force of who exactly you are supposed and desire to be! You cannot grow without making mistakes and taking risks; but you cannot grow, either, if you are carrying all the guilt and shame of your last mistake. Learn, forgive yourself, and let go.

Here are the steps I have been using in the last few years for own my decisions with a resounding YES and total satisfaction:

1. When deciding on something important and need a second set of eyes or a different mind, seek advice from whomever you trust. It can be one, two or more people, but I suggest limiting it to two people max to avoid more confusion.

2. Write all of their opinions/ideas down and then chunk them into bite sizes (go through them one by one).

3. Take all the other people who gave you advice/opinions out of this step completely and remain with your heart and opinions.

4. Based on how you feel, the opinions already given to you, what you had in mind prior to the opinions, potential pros and cons, then ask yourself how true are you to your decision?

5. This step is probably the most important of all. Ask yourself, "Will I be able to bear the outcome if plans don't go as planned without blaming or pointing fingers at anybody?"

If you have taken all these steps and you answered YES to number five, then you are ready. It's yours! If you have taken time to weigh pros and cons and you still have a resounding YES, then you are ready! Congratulations!!

This is your life, and you are in the driver's seat; you control which direction you want to turn. Your life is a beautiful story regardless of the trauma and the scratch marks in it, and you alone hold the pen and paper to write it because you know what is best, my friend. Life is about phases and chapters; you alone can decide what your next chapter will be. Your life is a movie playing out, and you are the main character because it is your story, my girl. Your life is a very empowering speech, and you are the powerful keynote speaker. Take charge!

6

Secret Six
The Gold During Turmoil

"All change is hard at first, messy in the middle and gorgeous at the end."

-Robin S. Sharma, The 5 AM Club: Own Your Morning. Elevate Your Life.

I understand when we think of crisis our negative defence mechanism automatically becomes activated because we as human beings immediately see danger; however, crisis can sometimes be a good thing. See, life is all about graduating from one dimension to another, but in between you must go through the examination to graduate. Although I haven't spent many years in school, I cannot recall even one student who loved exams so much that they did not stress a bit around exams time. But I can tell you about hundreds of students who were extremely excited about their next chapter after graduation. Change inspires growth. Do not limit yourself in the box; get out, try new things, and choose positivity even during a crisis. Look for opportunities in it.

Being an immigrant myself has given me another appreciation for all immigrants who leave their countries -- not because they voluntarily want too, but because they are forced due to whatever reasons out of their control, such as war, genocides, hate, and other insecurities. Some even start migrating the day they are born because parents choose to. Their children must then live in three to five countries, calling each one their home, while adapting to that new culture and way of living. I also admire those ambitious immigrants, and anyone who voluntarily moves miles away from home, who leaves their comfort zone and everything behind to start anew in pursue their dreams.

To truly thrive in this life, you must learn to embrace crisis, for in crisis, the truth of who you are is revealed. As you have seen, my journey hasn't been a very desirable one. As a little girl, those early childhood traumas were not things I caused or called for, but now that I am older and my story is with me for life, I decided to use my crises as a tool to amplify my voice and inspire others. I desire for it to change a life or two versus keeping myself in the "why me" zone (victimizing myself), which doesn't serve anyone and only brings me more grief.

There is no way you can explore your wings, your potential, or your capabilities if you are still stuck in your old ways. Or stuck in what everyone has done or said to you. You cannot afford to fear taking a leap of faith or fear doing that thing that you always wanted to do because you don't know how it's going to turn out or what they will say.

Originally, my heart desired to inspire single moms and teen moms, but I didn't want to mention anything about my childhood or my journey to motherhood. I didn't want my book to have anything to do with my childhood trauma. I wanted to inspire single moms using my adulthood struggles because that is what most of my adulthood had really been. I felt many women would relate and feel inspired, but I was wrong. Our childhood is our foundation. By wanting to inspire other women as a mom and only share how to thrive as a mom without sharing my "why" left people hanging. When I first reached out to my coach for help and guidance on book writing, we talked for ninety minutes. The purpose of the initial call was to help me understand what kind of book I wanted to write, why it was important to me, and what impact I wanted it to have on single moms and teen moms. During the call, she instructed me to write a letter to myself, which I agreed to. She also said, "After you do it, you can either burn it or mail the letters of forgiveness to those who have hurt you, letting them know that you forgive them."

I immediately started writing after our call.

Sistergirl, that day I sat on the computer straight for more than nine hours to finish this letter to myself while re-releasing those who hurt me. I say re-releasing them because I had already done it in my mind but hadn't written it down. I was so tense that I did not even use a bathroom or eat; I just did not feel hungry or tired. I cried through it from start to finish as I re-released every single person.

While writing these letters, I was in the basement of our then townhouse we were renting. One by one, my three children came down to check on me, wiped my tears asking me if I was okay, and kissed my acne-filled left cheek while tears and boogers dripped down. I revisited my childhood memories that I very much avoid talking about. I missed my grandmother, who was my only good childhood memory, even more during this process. I saw that little girl seeking attention from older men who had no empathy for her. I saw that little girl who felt rejected over and over. I also saw that little girl who lost her virginity against her will before she even had breast. I re-released and forgave everybody that I could think of that may have contributed to my scars, including myself for allowing them to hurt me even as an adult who should have known better. I revisited the morning where my once world became my nightmare with my ex.

I finally finished it and even shared it with my coach and posted a picture of my bloodshot eyes and puffy face from crying so much on my Facebook account. At first, I didn't understand why she asked me to do this, but she had a plan. This was another healing moment for me. It was another chance to face the truth I had been avoiding – that of my truth and my story. The truth shaped me into the woman I am today, and it has always been a subconscious factor in my decision-making and the people I gave control over my life.

During our following session, she started with prayers. She said she rarely does that, but felt called to do so before she told me what has been on her mind since our last session. After prayers, she proceeded to say, "Rebecca, I know you are very stubborn and don't want to talk about your childhood story and your pregnancy, but I really feel that you have a special connection with single moms and are in a position to connect and change their lives. I know you are withholding back so much of who you are and your 'why'. You can decide on how much you want to share, but you should really think about sharing a little bit more of who you are."

I told her she had a good point and I would think about it. After this session, I locked my bedroom door, sat down on my bed with Celine Dion playing in the background and two big scented candles lighting up my room. I contemplated on what to share and what not to share. After considering everything, I decided to share much more, especially from my early years, which is very crucial for any child.

Keep in mind, I didn't hold back for fear of what others thought. I was holding back because I was afraid of how my family would react. I didn't want to ruin our relationship after all the work we had all contributed to its repair. I didn't want anyone feeling thrown out into the world. I feared a crisis from sharing my story because I was specifically identifying the key players of my experience. But I knew this was my story and I needed to own it. I decided to take a leap of faith and reminded myself that this is my story, not theirs, and I should be allowed to do what I want with it. I lived it. I felt it. It cost me so much and it has left me many scars that will last a lifetime. With that, I decided to take a leap of faith and share my upbringing in this book.

No matter how strong or brave we may be, fear has its way of holding us hostage and sabotaging us from living our truth. It has its way of making us feel bad to share ourselves with the world, but you just have to take a leap of faith. Change can strengthen our character; it helps unveil things that are crucial as we work on becoming our authentic selves.

Speaking of change, did you see how COVID19 turned the world upside down and forced change on everybody worldwide? Schools closed, churches closed, companies closed, restaurants closed, night clubs closed, borders closed, and families (even parents and their children) in separate houses could not visit one other, even on special occasions. Weddings were put on hold, vacations were cancelled, kids couldn't play outside or go for a bike ride, many lives were lost, governments were scrambling, parents had to learn to homeschool for the first time in their lives, thousands of jobs were lost, yet there were also people who made millions of dollars as well. There were those who used this time to write books, and there were those who used this time to get in shape even with gyms closed. There were those who learned coding, there were those who used this time to expand their knowledge or learn a new skill. But there were also those who used this crisis as an excuse to sleep all day, drink themselves to sleep, watch Netflix from the moment they woke up to the moment they went to sleep and many ate themselves to the grave. What did you do during this crazy world pandemic? If the coronavirus pandemic didn't shift your world too much, then which life-changing crisis did you go through and how did you use it to your benefit? What will you do better if a crisis like this arises again?

This is a good example to demonstrate how sometimes changes are unavoidable and you will have to face them. What matters the most is how you will come out of it, how you think through it, and your ability to see past where you are sitting in that moment. I get it -- crises are hard and can be nerve-wrecking sometimes, especially when we have our set schedules and ways of doing things; however, we live in times of uncertainty and we must be ready and willing to embrace change as it is something that we can't escape.

Next time, when you have to make a tough decision to leave that job you just hate so you can pursue your calling, to walk away from an abusive relationship, to pack your things and move to find a cheaper place so you can save up some money, or when you have to travel to a foreign country to help the less fortunate, know that you are not alone. Making the move or even thinking of the move isn't easy, but if you go back to gratitude, focus on end the result and your deeper *why*, it opens a window of opportunities and growth.

Growth can come from anywhere during each season of life. Hurricanes happen, pandemics happen, death takes away the people we cherish, tornadoes destroy, losses happen, and yes, it is hard, but the truth is that life is all about stages and seasons. Changes occur year-round and we are always moving through them; we just do not realize it or pay much attention to it. Think of how many stages you have gone through since you were born to this day. Crawling, walking, adolescence to adulthood, and then into motherhood. You enjoyed some better than others, you learned different things in each stage, but you lived through them and survived or even thrived.

Let us look at weather seasons. We have summer, winter, spring, and fall. You may not have all these four seasons in your state or country, but you have a rainy and sunny season. I can almost guarantee you enjoy one of these seasons better than the other, but you still find a way to live through the other and have fun. My question to you is: Can you do the same when other non-exciting seasons of life come your way? How can you prepare yourself? What can you do to support yourself through an unpleasant season?

Be solution and results-oriented while you live in whichever stage or season you're currently experiencing, so you have something to harvest when the temporary season is over. Take a crisis as a planting season just like a farmer (people still had to eat even during the world pandemic). Take this season as a preparation period, just like a bride preparing for her big day in coming months. Take this time to expand on your knowledge to put yourself a few steps ahead when the crisis is over (do not forget that people pay for knowledge and skills, not just a pretty face and a killer shape or sweet words). I want you to look at a crisis like an entrepreneur and begin imagining what you could learn or how you could grow during this time. There have never been better times to pivot like the times we are in.

Sistergirl, crisis can force you to sort and realize your priorities in the bigger picture. That's one of its blessings. For instance, after COVID19 hit, I was scared like everyone else. I was asking questions that rarely had answers, but I had to make one especially important decision: do I stop my two jobs for a bit or not? I decided to stop both of my jobs so I could be home to comfort my children in one of the craziest times of their lives. This wasn't an easy decision to make as a single mom, as the only breadwinner for my household, and I knew this would cause me a lot more financial discomfort, but I also knew it was the best thing I could do for myself and my children during that season. I realized children, who don't always express how they feel, were also panicking and confused. My children needed me to comfort them, which my two jobs would not have allowed me to do working fourteen to sixteen hours a day. They were stuck in the house and needed me to cook and clean a little more than usual. They had no school to go to and I now had to become their teacher. I also worried about bringing the virus home to my children, to which I was not willing to take a chance. Stopping both jobs cut my income by more than half, and yes, I had to make some radical changes in my accommodation and how I spent money. However, this break allowed me to bond with my children and comfort them. I needed them to rest assured knowing they come above everything else and can count on me even during a crisis. I needed them to know and trust that mummy is ready and willing to drop everything to ensure they are okay both physically, emotionally, and mentally. I had to sort my priorities between work and family. I understand this may not be possible for everybody, and I was grateful for the opportunity to be there for my children.

Life is full of surprises and uncertainty, but we still must continue navigating this thing called life and its unforeseen events. I whole-heartedly believe that to truly be capable of pushing on and living a happy life, especially in uncertain times, we must get out of our own head, look around us for precious things to be grateful for, and learn how to look for opportunities in the season. Problems, disappointments, betrayals, and other unexciting events are things that started at the beginning of human creation and it will remain until the end. We must understand that we are not the first ones to experience whatever we are going through and that it is just another phase in life that is passing by. We must look at these situations as a growth season. You lighten up your own journey when you look at a crisis as an opportunity season and give thanks that you get to take part in life.

As an example, I desired to write a book in 2014 but never really acted upon it; it was just a wish. In 2019, I attended a book writing event hosted by Gerry Robert & Black Card Books. I will never forget this event. During this event, I asked a question and Gerry responded, saying, "You could be next Lisa Nichols." I looked on my right at an ambitious, well-spoken, handsome young man, and who would later become my friend, thinking Gerry was talking to him. Gerry pointed directly at me and clarified he was talking to me. This excited and pumped me up because I just love Lisa and look up to her as a speaker who changes lives -- including mine! While I did not want to become Lisa, I wanted to become a better version of myself and make a huge impact on women through my story, just like Lisa Nichols.

When the coronavirus pandemic took over the entire world, I was forced to stop work to be home with my children. I now saw an opportunity to finally write my book (since I now had 24-hours at my disposal)!

It wasn't a smooth ride.

I had just put almost my entire savings into my RRSP and locked it into the GIC before I had stopped working. I needed to come up with over three thousand dollars for book coaching. Kids needed to eat and we still needed a roof over our heads. I had other bills to pay, and I didn't want to pay the 20 percent withholding tax and bank fees, but I knew it was now or never. Although I was concerned about my grammar, and didn't know where I would get all the things to write the entire book about, I decided and told myself, "I am writing a book no matter what. I need to maximize this time." Of course, as a high school dropout and a single mother of three, deciding to hire a book coach during a world crisis and taking on writing a book was nerve- wrecking -- but I knew it had to be done now.

Before we continue, I want to warn you. Don't think when opportunities come or when you find opportunities during a crisis that everything will go smoothly. In fact, your life may look a little more chaotic than it already was; however, you must find things to be thankful during the crisis so you can keep holding on and pressing through.

Immediately after executing a deal with a book coach and my money locked up, I faced other challenges that led me to find alternative accommodation. While other people were home isolating and keeping safe, I was busy moving up and down. I spent hours on Kijiji looking for a rental property to move into. I had to pack our entire three bedrooms town house in just two weeks and move. I had to come up with five hundred dollars to pay movers as well as a storage unit. I had to come up with Plan B and turned to a friend for help. The friend agreed, but I had to share a double bed with my two boys for three weeks. As a 210lbs girl, this meant I couldn't turn in the night and that caused me terrible back pain (and I already had back issues). I fell off the bed most nights because the bed was too small. I would sometimes ask one of my boys to sleep with his head facing down by my legs (criss-cross/upside down).

During my stay at my friend's house, writing was a battle that not everyone could win since the room was too small for my desk. I had to use the dining table to write, so I would move my desktop computer downstairs each morning, up at mealtimes, then back down after meals, up when guests came, down when they left, and then up each evening again. Top it off with my laptop being stolen a few months prior. I would move them to the dining table to do my both my research and writing, which wasn't easy as there were usually guests even though we were in pandemic, or the TV was loud in the background from wake-up to bed-time, or the kitchen vent was going, or my friend wanted to talk till late at night.

After the three-week stay with my friend, we temporarily moved into a two-bedrooms student residency on a nearby collage, which is where I continued writing and eventually completed this book! Even with all this chaos, I knew this was a planting season. This was a preparation season, and there was no way I would waste this opportunity with my well-planned lies and excuses, if I wanted to be able to harvest in the coming season. I had every excuse to throw in blankets and say forget it, but I saw an opportunity and I had to hold on to my desire to be the agent of change in single mom's lives. As tough as changes or crises are, they are needed to help us discover who we truly are, our capabilities, and our hidden talents.

Crises enables us to discover things we like that we would otherwise have never even dream of. We suddenly learn how to deal with pressure, which is a crucial skill in life. Sometimes we don't know our strength because we have been put down far too many times, have been led to not believe in ourselves, or it is because we have been comfortable for too long. Maybe we feel afraid to fail or feel we'd be laughed at.

Believe it or not, crises can also boost our belief and attitude towards certain things we felt afraid of or had been avoiding. From book writing, I now know I can write one hundred more books if I decide to do so. I probably would not have said that before. Amazing opportunities to grow and learn abound each time you go through any sort of change or crisis. I am not saying that we should wish for crises, but we can change how we look at it by shifting our mindset from problem-view to a solution-view.

A crisis is a temporary situation; it's a phase in life that isn't here to stay. Now let me ask you something: What good would it do to respond to a temporary situation with a permanent solution? Why would you let the crisis run, ruin, or dictate the rest of your life? Crises are like seasons that shake you up a bit, test you, and help you shift. Take them with grace.

Ask yourself, "What can I plant in this season that I could harvest in the upcoming season?" No matter what situation you are in, it will come to an end soon; it's a preparation for grander things.

Do not let the crises run your life, my friend. Do not sweat small things. There is always a solution. Need work? Find a problem that you can solve and sell it to others. Need a new opportunity? Learn a new skill or deepen another skill that can give you an advantage in your current career.

I don't know about you, but for me -- it's either I die trying or live to tell the story; I refuse to be pushed back or controlled.

7

Secret Seven
Celebrating Your Accomplishments and Those of Others

CELEBRATING YOUR MINOR OR MAJOR ACHIEVEMENTS

"The more you praise and celebrate your life,
the more there is in life to celebrate."
-Oprah Winfrey

Being your authentic self is an inside job that requires constant reminders and intention to ensure we do not fall off the wagon, and I am a firm believer that there is no better reminder than celebrating who we are and all the amazing things we have accomplished.

There are endless benefits for taking time to recognize and celebrate your achievements, big or small. Sometimes, there are benefits that we rarely think of. This act can boost your wellbeing and confidence. It fuels and energizes you. Celebrating your minor achievements motivates you to pursue greater achievements. It inspires others as well and gives you a sense of fulfilment.

When you are busy sweeping through your goals, your to-do lists, and other various demands of life, especially as a single mama, it is quite easy to overlook your small wins. I highly encourage you to take the time to see how hard you have been working and acknowledge how much you have done. Celebrating your wins gives you a chance to reflect and recognize what is working and what you can do better.

You inspire others when you celebrate yourself. It's encouraging and motivates them to start what they have been wanting to do. I know I felt inspired when my friend from the book writing event published his first book! I reached out to congratulate him, and we talked about many things, including future business endeavours and collaborations.

I have had so many wins in my life, but my first big win, apart from having my children, was when I graduated from my personal Support Worker program with honours. I am aware that a personal support worker diploma may mean nothing to others, but it meant the world to me for various reasons. I was an elementary school dropout (was in and out). I was a high school dropout and my last grade at the time was ninth. I had failed my family. I had failed my admission test twice, which meant I only had one last chance left to start this program. Can you feel the pressure I was under as a hungry twenty-three-year-old single mother of three small children? If I hadn't passed the last time, I would have had to wait to go back in three months. Hearing "three months" sounded like ten years.

Shortly after I was accepted into college, I became heartbroken. I started college on January 14, 2013, and by February 14, 2013, my relationship with my best friend ended because he felt I didn't have time for him anymore between school and children. I was tired of being on social assistance and begging different agencies for casual labour jobs. I was ready and willing to spend nights studying after my babies went to bed. I was willing to be vulnerable enough to ask my amazing friends for help with studying (Ruth, Lissy, and Shannon, thank you so much!) because I needed all the help I could get. I was willing to look stupid in class and ask Miss B. all the questions I did not understand, and even stayed after school so she could help me. I was willing to beg my sisters to help babysit so I could study. I was crazy enough to ask my friend to help me bribe her daughters to babysit. I am glad I did.

I made a bold move, and many thought I was wasting my time. They believed there was no way I would ever do it. I ask you, Sistergirl, are you believing in yourself and how great you could be or are you believing other people's opinions of how great they think you cannot be? I grew up believing how great I couldn't be. I was raised to believe I literally can't do anything because I am a girl. Then, once it clicked within my heart that this wasn't true, I dropped those beliefs like hot potatoes, and I've never been the same since.

Not only graduating, but graduating with honours gave me the wings I needed. It amplified a voice that was often abated by other people's opinions, and it gave me a voice that wasn't only to be used for me. I have been using this voice to advocate for people with physical and developmental disabilities who are often overlooked, bypassed, and not given the opportunities they deserve in our society. This diploma has opened a whole lot of doors that I would otherwise never have dream of. I have and will achieve greater things in this life, but this diploma remains my biggest achievement as this is where my wings came from, and I will forever celebrate it. It brought me freedom and opened to me the world of possibilities.

From this day, I have learned that as long as you are willing to step out in faith, hold on a little longer even during a crisis (like starting school and ending a relationship with my best friend of many years), and be your own greatest cheerleader, even the sky in not a limit. Think of the end results as a motivating factor (what this will do for you, your children, the voiceless, and whatever is your driving force if you don't give up), then you can do anything you put your mind to and time on.

My bold moves and persistence have enabled me to encourage many more people to shoot for stars. I have touched many lives, who have become so dear to my heart, through my work and my personal experiences. In return, I have also learned a lot, and if I were to do it all over again, I wouldn't hesitate.

HOW YOU CAN CELEBRATE BOTH YOUR BIG OR SMALL ACHIEVEMENTS.

- Throw yourself a party for that massive win

- Go for dinner to your favourite restaurant

- Hit the dance floor with your besties

- Treat yourself to a spa day

- Go for a massage

- Take a vacation or even just a day trip somewhere special

- Grab popcorn or your favourite snack and watch a movie with your family or friends

- Buy yourself a nice gift or buy something you have been wanting to buy, but couldn't afford

- Go hiking or skiing

- Pop a bottle of champagne or wine and take a nice long bubble bath

- Cook your favourite meal or bake your favourite dessert

- Take a day off cooking and order in

- Share the good news and pay it forward!

CELEBRATING OTHERS

Sistergirl, we just talked about how beneficial it is to celebrate your wins, and I hope it was very exciting. I am confident that you will make a point to celebrate yourself. However, there are numerous benefits in celebrating other people's wins as well.

It takes maturity and practice to fully embrace other people's success, especially when it feels like they signed a "lucky" contract with God while you feel like everything is just slipping through your hands like water. The benefits are so worth it when you can fully love on your family and friend's accomplishments.

Yes, I just told you about my biggest achievement and while the majority of people thought I was wasting my time and government's money, there were other people who believed in me and celebrated me. There were people who listened when I needed to vent, and I will forever be thankful to them.

Celebrating others creates a safe space for everyone. It replaces bitterness, frustration, and resentment. It replaces jealousy with joy, freedom, and happiness. When you sincerely and enthusiastically celebrate your family or friends, it also opens up a learning opportunity for you. You can pick their brain to see how they did it, so you too can follow the steps if that's your desire. Family and friendships are all about sharing your ups and downs, and I genuinely believe there is no greater way to nourish a relationship than joyfully celebrating family members and friends on their achievements. Doing so creates an environment of open communication, and they will celebrate you when it is your turn.

I am sure you may be wondering, "How do I celebrate my family and friends or show them I am happy for them, Rebecca?"

It is remarkably simple. You do not have to spend money on a big party or go clubbing if that's not how you want it. You certainly don't need to spend crazy amounts of money on gifts, either. Here are some options:

- You can post about them on your social media with a nice caption so your friends can help you celebrate their achievement.

- You can make them a gift yourself.

- You can call them or text them to tell them how proud of them you are.

- You can send them a handwritten note.

- You can invite them over for dinner.

- You can take them out for lunch, dinner, or coffee.

- If they are hosting a party, you can show up with a gift or a card.

- You can drop off flowers at their work or home.

There is no wrong or right way. Just do whatever is within your means and feels right for you. What matters is the gesture and the thought, not the amount or method.

REFLECTION

1. Think of a moment you felt accomplished. What was the accomplishment?

2. Now, in two sentences, explain how you felt when you were celebrating this accomplishment by yourself or with friends.

3. What did you do to help you accomplish that? What inspired you to keep going?

4. Now, name three people you can celebrate today. They do not have to accomplish anything; you can celebrate them by appreciating them for being part of your life.

5. How will you show your appreciation for them? Keep it sweet, simple, and fun!

BONUS SECRET

The Power of Giving

While you celebrate your wins and friend's wins, don't forget to extend a helping hand to the less fortunate.

I cannot stress this enough. People often confuse giving with being rich or having "enough." There is no greater gift in life than giving. I also want to place heavy emphasis on the point that we all have something special to give. Before you entertain a thought that you have nothing to give, let me reassure you that you do. I will not spend too much time on this because the chances are you have received something from somebody, and you know how it made you feel. We all love receiving, but not too many put much thought toward giving.

Let me be clear that I am not just talking about giving back and forth with your wealthy friends. While that is great, too, I am specifically talking about paying it forward and blessing someone in need.

I am not sure about you, but giving gives me another level of fulfilment that is just out of this world. The beautiful part is that even my children know the beauty of giving and love it as well. Most of us expect Christmas gifts, birthday gifts, and so on, but that is because we have someone or somewhere to expect them from. We as parents go all out and spend crazy amounts of money on toys, books, video games, and activities for our children, but can't we spare $5 a week, or at least a month, to help a hungry child whose dream for Christmas is to just get a plate of food?

A few years ago, my daughter was gift shopping through her school for our family, and she knew I loved jewellery. (Jewellery, mugs, candles, notebooks, and pens are typical gifts my children get me. They know me too well.) She had also been observing my other interests; I didn't know she was observing because she was only eleven years at the time. Somehow, she knew I had supported One Woman in the past and had spoken highly about them.

The One Woman website describes its mission as:

> One Woman is a global social enterprise on a mission to help women and girls around the globe live their dreams and reach their full potential through education, skills training, and entrepreneurship. We believe that all women are born with incredible gifts to share with the world and make each of our communities a better place. Our goal is to provide the tools, educational opportunities, support and encouragement to empower women to become all that they dream to be.

I had one of my Rafiki bracelets hanging off the mirror of my dresser, so as I got ready each morning I was reminded of the impact I am making. I see it as fuel to do even more. I also had another one of those bracelets in my car hanging on my rear-view mirror since I spend so much time in my car. (Rafiki is a Swahili word for "friend", which is handmade with love by a woman in Kenya. Her business is empowering her to earn a living and create a better future for her family and her community.)

She had already asked me about them a while back, but I had not really thought much about it. I thought it was just another question; you know kids can really ask! So, she was at school shopping for me and Lord behold, she spotted the Rafiki bracelets and according to her, "I jumped to them and quickly grabbed them because I knew you really liked them." She bought three of them in different colours and was just as thrilled to buy them for me as much as I was thrilled to receive them. They are more than just bracelets because when I look at them, I know another woman was able to feed her family that night.

Can you imagine? How can we raise change-makers if we ourselves are not leading by example?

One evening, I was tired from writing because I had been writing for a few hours and decided to take the kids for a treat (just to get a feel of a different environment and go for a nice evening drive to catch up). On our way, we saw this big man with long hair, wearing a filthy, dirty hat, camouflage shorts, and a black t-shirt holding a cup and sitting somewhere by a poll on a sidewalk between the two streets. I saw his clothing and hair, but something else stuck out to one of my sons (my middle child, Barak).

He shouted, "Mummy, look at that guy. He has stitches by his eye, and I think he is homeless. I feel bad for him."

I responded, "Wow, that's sad."

Then my son said, "Maybe he doesn't have money because of Coronavirus. Mom, do you have change?"

Because we were stopped at the red light, I looked and surely, I did not have change. I told him, "Maybe on our way back." We carried on and continued with our drive. On our way back, as we were approaching the place, I asked all of my children to vote if we should turn to go give that guy some change if he is still there or if we should just go straight home.

All three voted loudly, "Turn, please!"

We turned and surely the poor guy was still there, and we were able to spare him some change!

Do you want to know something? That night, while we sat on my bed taking turns to mention three things we were thankful for (this is our usual ritual when I'm home at bedtime), the first thing Barak said when it was his turn was, "I am very thankful that we could help that homeless guy. I feel bad for him."

Can you imagine at ten years old, during a pandemic, spending all day in the house with your little brother who gets on your nerves and a sister who can, at times, be a bit bossy -- that this is what he was thankful for? He could have been thankful for his PS4. He could have been thankful for food or TV, but the first thing out of his mouth to be thankful for was that we helped somebody! Think about it!

You may be wondering how I do this. There are tons of ways you can do this act of giving. You can give your time by babysitting for a friend or a neighbour (to give them a break or a chance to focus on their school assignment). You can donate your time by volunteering with your favourite charity organization. You can offer emotional support or respite for the elderly in your community. (It is emotionally and physically draining for caregivers, especially when their loved one has dementia.) You can feed the homeless or start/partake in a food drive. You can offer physical support to the elderly and the sick in your community, or even family and friends, by cutting grass or running errands for them. You can give your knowledge by sharing it or mentoring/tutoring students in low-income neighbourhoods who can't afford to pay a tutor. You can offer time to tell stories at the library so that parents can get a little break. You can give money by donating to your favourite charity or one that aligns with your values. You can give financial help to family and friends who need a little extra support. (This is personal for me. I don't know what I would have done in many situations without my family and close friends.)

The list is endless of amazing gestures you can do to pay it forward. There are endless benefits to giving. Giving is a self-declaration of divine abundance; it's a law of attraction. I give because I will always have enough. Let us shout to the world that we will never lack by giving what we can of ourselves.

Watch as the art of giving boosts your self-esteem. Watch as it boosts your sense of fulfilment. Watch as it boosts the empowerment of others as well as yourself.

I can honestly and confidently say that once you master the art of giving, you never lack.

Giving is something so personal and for me, it is glued in my bones and veins because I have been on the spectrum of receiving at the lowest and most desperate moments as well as experiencing the beauty of giving. I have experienced both worlds, and I will never ever forget those who have come to my rescue when I was at my lowest, even though they did not know what I was going through. It's not the amount that counts, it's the thought put into it.

Whose world will you change today?

BONUS SECRET

Jennifer Ramirez

YOU ARE NOT ALONE AND IT'S NOT TOO LATE TO RECLAIM WHAT'S YOURS.

The Importance of Empowering Women, Jennifer Ramirez

Please allow me to introduce to you another powerhouse of a woman who, despite facing sexual abuse at age seven by a trusted family member, getting entangled in gang relationships, and clubbing her life away, was able to reclaim her life through positive thinking and hard work. This message of empowerment is the foundation of her guidance with all the women she is privileged to support and guide through her women-empowerment events and coaching. Despite sexual abuse and a series of adversities, Jennifer shares how she stopped being the victim and took charge of her destiny. Through personal stories, she demonstrates how you can reclaim your life with positive thinking and hard work.

Jennifer Ramirez is the founder and executive director of & Rise., a non-profit organization that helps women become the ultimate versions of themselves through community and a sisterhood of like-minded women.

IN HER WORDS

My name is Jennifer Ramirez and I am a single mother and a sexual abuse survivor. At the age of seven, I was abused by a close family member. The trauma affected me negatively; I became angry and resentful. It was only last year, at the age of thirty-three, that I began openly talking about my sexual abuse. I did not realize that all my poor decisions, toxic relationships, my lack of self-confidence, and anger resulted from my past trauma.

My twenties were the hardest years of my life. I had my daughter at twenty-one years old, which forced me to grow up faster. I stopped listening to that little voice inside, eventually. For the first five years of my daughter's life, her father's mother helped me with her, so I had every other weekend free. This is when I began clubbing and partying hard because I felt lost. I did not care about the consequences of my actions. As responsible as I was with my daughter, I was equally irresponsible with myself. I did not love myself. I had low self-esteem, which showed in the type of people I surrounded myself with, the men I used to date, and how I treated myself.

I used to have a bad-boy fetish. I used to date drug dealers and was in two serious relationships with gang members. It was cute in the early stages of my twenties but once I hit about twenty-five, I grew out of it, thank God! Since things with my daughter's father did not work out, I was constantly searching for that man to "complete" me and my family. Society tells us we aren't normal unless both parents are in the picture, so I was always seeking normalcy. I used to choose dysfunctional and toxic men. I always had relationship drama and I honestly started to think it was normal.

I used to work in a toxic work environment for about seven years and lived in a gang-infested neighbourhood in Chicago. Negativity seemed to be all around me. I was poor, living paycheck-to-paycheck, and barely making ends meet. Sometimes, I had to decide if I was buying groceries or buying gas to get to work that week. The only way for me to stay afloat was through credit cards. I racked up over $25,000 in credit card debt and I was drowning. I had zero financial support from my daughter's father, which added to my financial struggle.

I walked around with a negative attitude. I became such a toxic person that I didn't even get along with my family anymore. I have a twin sister with whom I have always been close to, and even she and I didn't speak a lot at that point in time. I was a different person. I was so angry; I carried it with me everywhere I went. I attracted people like me -- negative and angry.

When I was twenty-five years old, my thought process began to change. I knew the way I was living my life was not working. I grew tired of being poor. I grew tired of being unhappy. I grew tired of being with men who did not value me. I was just tired of everything! I wanted a better life, but I didn't know how to make that happen. All I knew: if I wanted a different outcome in life, then I would have to make different decisions. A different mindset can be life changing and that is exactly what happened for me. Once I started thinking more positively and began listening to that little voice inside, my transformation began.

In 2012, I decided to buy my first condo, which was a huge accomplishment! I also was promoted to a new job and I loved everything about it! It was everything opposite of my previous work environment. I had an amazing, supportive boss and great co-workers, which was truly inspiring! My boss encouraged me to take a college level Excel course, which motivated me to stay in school. I ended up obtaining my Associate's degree in 2017, and during that time, I also began saving money and continued to pay down my debt. By the time I was thirty, I was 100 percent debt free! With no debt and extra money, I decided to be a landlord and purchase another condo! I felt scared, but was willing to take the risk because I was tired of being poor!

Two years later, I purchased another house, and I was now a landlord, twice over. Additionally, I consciously began doing things that made me happy and I decided to stop dating entirely. All those toxic relationships taught me so many valuable lessons about myself, what I deserve, and what I would no longer tolerate from a man. Taking time away from men and dating was a game changer for me as the living on my own helped me grow on so many different levels.

I also began blogging, which motivated me to become an author. I also started an Air B&B business with a partner to create another stream of income for myself. In the beginning of 2020, I sold my first condo which allowed me to quit my 9-to-5 job. It was definitely scary, but I knew in my heart that I had to chase my destiny. I wanted to focus my time and attention on the nonprofit organization I created. A few months after quitting my job, I graduated from college (after seven long years of working full-time and going to school part-time)! It can be done! It wasn't easy, but it was definitely worth it.

At one point, I went with a friend to a networking event and all the women sat in a circle and began talking about their lives, struggles, passions, and dreams. This was the first time I had been to an event that made me feel hopeful, and I left feeling completely inspired! I wanted other women to have the same experience that I had that night, and I began hosting women's empowerment events in my living room. In October 2019, I threw my first big event and we sold out 150 tickets on Eventbrite. This is where I had my light bulb moment. The amount of interest made me realize there was a demand for these events, and the feedback blew me away, so I created a nonprofit organization called &Rise.

&Rise empowers women to be the ultimate versions of themselves, no matter what adversities they have faced. We believe in community, sisterhood, and thoughtful storytelling so other women can see they aren't alone in their struggles. We have an amazing community of supportive and kind women who have each other's back! The story behind the &Rise logo is the "&" means there is more to tell, your story is not over yet. The "rise" means rising above and overcoming any adversities you have endured.

&Rise offers personal and professional development workshops, women's empowerment events, and weekly support groups for women who are sexual and domestic abuse survivors. At &Rise, we want women to leave our events better than how they came in. We want you to know that you can accomplish anything and can make your own dreams come true with the right mindset, hard work, and commitment. The profit from our event ticket sales go directly to women in need. Our plan for &Rise is to make it a global organization to help women all around the world. Our vision is to support single mothers who desire to go to college, with financial assistance for tuition, supplies, and childcare. Additionally, we help sexual and domestic abuse survivors with free therapy and counselling to overcome trauma-related mental and emotional blocks so they can rise above to be the ultimate versions of themselves.

I also am a life and business coach and am the CEO of &Flourish, where I help single mom entrepreneurs break free from their toxic past to kick stress, insecurity, and fear so they can create their dream business and a life they love! I offer one-on-one coaching, group coaching, and mastermind workshops. I love the mastermind workshops because it brings so much value to women in their businesses while also allowing them to network in a meaningful way. My goal is to make sure everyone reaches the finish line, together!

I have a soft spot for single mothers because I know how hard it is. Everyone says they "know" being a single parent is hard, but in reality, they don't really know the daily struggles we face. I know what it feels like to feel alone and helpless. I understand the financial, emotional, and mental struggles with raising a child alone. I want &Rise to be the resource women turn to when they need help. I never understood why I was sexually abused by someone who was supposed to protect me or why I had to raise a child on my own. Now I know that my trauma has brought me here, to this point in my life, to help other women. I now know I went through so much heartbreak, disappointment, and struggle because it humbled and motivated me to help people who need inspiration in their lives.

Empowerment is important for our self-esteem. Having a community where other people are positive, kind, understanding, and inspiring can be life changing for women who do not have a support system. Feeling strong fuels our confidence. When I tell you that you can accomplish anything and share stories of other women who have done it, it is extremely powerful. When we empower one another, as women, we support our understanding of the skills we have while also bringing out skills hidden within.

Naturally, women are caretakers. We tend to put everyone else's needs above our own and do not want to trouble others with our personal issues, so we keep it inside. This is especially true of single mothers; we are used to being highly self-sufficient and are less likely to let anyone know we need help. When women have a community where we can safely voice our personal and professional concerns, it helps us grow. Going through life struggles alone can be emotionally and mentally damaging, so a community is truly essential.

As empowered women, we are less likely to accept being mistreated. Mistreatment includes domestic violence and sexual exploitation, even in a marriage. When we feel powerful, we understand what unacceptable behaviour is, what should not be tolerated, and what to do about it.

Helping single mothers with their college education is important because feeling proud and accomplished can make you feel as if you can do anything thereafter. This inner-strength then enables us to empower people around us. I feel education is powerful, especially for the single mothers who feel hopeless or as if they will never get ahead in life.

Elevating women can also allow economic independence, which also contributes to the economic benefits of the household and society. When we are healthy, empowered, educated, and able to work, everyone wins. The health and wellbeing of women is closely linked to that of prosperous communities and nations. We women spend a lot of our money on things that directly benefit our families. We prioritize things like food, medicine, and education for our children. Mothers who had an education are more likely to send their kids to school than those mothers with no education because they know the importance of education. If we want a healthier and more productive world, then elevating women is a no-brainer. When we invest in women, we can make a difference in our community and in the world.

For the amazing woman reading this, I leave you with the following advice:

Set goals and write them down. You are more likely to achieve your goals by writing them. The act of writing your goals forces you to be clear on what to accomplish, which also plays a part in motivating you to complete the tasks necessary to get there.

Invest in yourself. Take professional and personal development courses to better your skills. Yes, some of these things cost money, but investing in your own growth is worth every penny. Developing yourself can benefit you personally and professionally.

Ask for help. If you need help but are too proud to ask, you are doing yourself a disservice. How is anyone supposed to help you if they do not know you need help? I made the mistake of feeling too proud to ask anyone for help when I was younger. I had this mentality where I expected people to ask me if I needed help, which was not wise. If you need help, let your support circle know. It would surprise you to know how willing people are to help if you simply ask.

Change the way you think. As you can see from my story, mindset is so important. When I was in a negative mindset, that was what I attracted and that is what my mind was limited to. Once I changed my perception and began thinking more positively, my life changed. Change starts with you.

You have to want it and be willing to work for it. My transformation did not happen overnight. It took years to get where I am today and the same transformation is possible for you, but the question is, how badly do you want it?

To learn more about &Rise and how we empower women or to receive our newsletters, please visit us at www.womenrisechicago.org. Follow &Rise on Facebook @womenrisechicago and Instagram @andrise_women. If you are interested in coaching or mastermind workshops, please visit andflourish.co or follow us on Instagram @andflourishco. To purchase my book *Passion, Purpose, and the Pursuit of Dreams,* please visit andflourish.bigcartel.com

What an amazing story. A terrible beginning, a victim mindset, and then a beautiful testimony to the wonders of positive thinking, humbling ourselves enough to ask for help, and working hard. We can turn our lives around for better!

Please don't forget to connect with Jennifer and grab your free 30-minute consultation complimentary session with her!

8

Secret Eight
Unleashing the Power of Vision

We all have powerful passions, talents, and skills able to unlock illimitable potential, but only a few really get to discover and use them. I am not sure what your faith is and while that isn't even the topic in this book, allow me to share with you a verse that spoke so loudly to me a few years ago:

> "Then the LORD told me: 'I will give you my message in the form of a vision. Write it clearly enough to be read at a glance.'" (Habakkuk 2:2).

> As if that wasn't powerful enough, it goes on to say: "Where there is no vision, the people perish" (Proverbs 29:18).

This is the turning point where you allow yourself to shine brightly and use your pain to make an impact. This is where you recycle your pain into purpose. This will require you to take a leap of faith and even get a little out of your comfort zone.

Let me start by asking you a few questions to reflect on: Are you fully satisfied with your job, the way they treat you, the pay, and the hours you work? Are you growing in your job or are you committed to staying in the same position for forty years until retirement or till you die? How is your pension plan there? Do you believe in their mission and vision? What do they stand for and would you continue associating with them if you had another option? If you could do your dream job, what would it be? What are you doing about it?

If you like your job and feel satisfied, then do you have a story about how you survived a nasty incident or overcame trauma that you feel could help others? Are you incredibly passionate about something that many of your family and friends keep asking you for help? What hand skills can you use for profit? Is there something you are incredibly good at that you could do to help even more people while earning a good income doing it? For those who are spiritual, what is one thing God has been whispering in your ear and you keep ignoring? If you could change something about your life today, what would it be?

The bigger questions are: Where do you see yourself in two years? Five years? How about ten years? What dreams will you be taking back with you to the grave that could have changed hundreds, thousands, or even millions of people? Are you okay with that or are you going to commit to you and your dreams, starting today?

One afternoon I took a break from writing and decided to browse Instagram.

As soon as I opened my Instagram, I kept seeing pictures of an exceptionally beautiful woman with a very contagious smile popping up on my timeline. Many Nigerian celebrities kept posting her with crying emojis, and as I kept scrolling through, I came to realize that this beautiful woman had died and those were tributes.

Being the curious person I am, I decided to Google her and even started watching a few of her interviews on YouTube. Not only was this woman's smile contagious, her heart was made of gold.

Her name was Ibidunni Elizabeth Ighodalo. She was the founder of the Ibidunni Ibidunni Ighodalo Foundation[5].

The foundation's mission statement:

> An organization on a mission to raise awareness about infertility and the challenges associated with it. To stop the stigmatization of couples dealing with infertility and to provide the spiritual, financial and psychological support they require. With a vision to to have every couple enjoy the gift of parenthood regardless of their financial or social status but the main focus is for those who cannot afford such treatment.

Ibidunni was also a former beauty queen, a co-pastor, and a wife of an exceedingly popular pastor in Nigeria. According to CNN Africa, she had been traveling across the country to build isolation centres for Coronavirus patients and died at age thirty-nine in her hotel room due to cardiac arrest. Her close friend told CNN Africa that she received a message from her friend (Ibidunni) on the night before her death where she talked about her birthday plans.

Her last message to a good friend was: "Sweetie, it's my 40th next month and I want to help 40 couples to have their babies... That's all I want. No party. No surprise. Nothing. I just want to make 40 homes happy."

Her story of turning her pain into purpose is why she has taken space in this book, and I am honoured to share her story with you.

According to the website:

> This foundation was borne out of her own personal struggles. A newly married couple in 2007, Ibidunni and her husband, Pastor Ituah Ighodalo, looked forward to starting their family and holding their children in their arms.
>
> However, they watched the years roll by without a child. After sev-

---

5 See references page for more information.

eral doctors' appointments, they were told that they wouldn't have children unless they sought treatment through assisted reproduction. This was the doctor's report they received, but Ibidunni and Pastor Ituah chose to believe God's own report. Unshaken in their faith, the couple firmly believed that they will carry their own children. This period of delay also came with pressure and a lot of insensitivity from people. Ibidunni had to deal with the emotions, pain, and the roller-coaster hormonal imbalance that came with all sorts of these treatments. Thankfully, Pastor Ituah was an amazing support system for her and was always there for her through all the procedures; unflinching by her side.

Along her fertility journey however, Ibidunni met women who only needed one round of a treatment to make their dreams come through (she had gone through nine). The only thing holding them back was either the lack of finance or the psychological support needed to get through it. It was at that point she decided to stop thinking about herself and start trusting God to help these couples fulfil their dreams of having their children.

While she wasn't a single mom or from a poor background, pain is pain, and I personally couldn't imagine any sharper pain than this. Can you imagine yourself in her shoes? And then taking it a step further to use your money and energy to help women so that they never have to feel what you are feeling? Now, that's what I call turning pain into purpose!

In her interviews, she said that in the beginning, she had to use her and her husband's money to pay for women before people eventually started supporting them (foundation) financially. This woman and her husband are a prime example of selflessness and what turning pain into purpose to serve others looks like.

You can learn more about this incredible woman and support the foundation at: https://ibidunniighodalofoundation.org/about-us/

Phone: +234 803 306 5708, +234 805 905 5555

Email: info@ibidunniighodalofoundation.org

Dreams do change over time due to many circumstances, age, and other things, and as we have just seen, this powerful woman's plans changed, but she refused to host a pity party. While things didn't go as planned, she refused to see her situation as a failure.

For me, it was crystal clear that, after going through what I've been through in my childhood, my teen pregnancy, motherhood, raising my children as a single mom, and living through till I eventually found my wings, that I wanted to help other moms, but I didn't know how. I lived it. I knew the pain and the void. I know what I would have wished to have had in those times. I know what it is like to be stomped down by someone else's words, and I wanted to inspire somebody using my story and experiences. A dream is not a wish, it's something with a deeper meaning to you that, come rain or shine, you will walk miles to do it!

REFLECTION

Something to ponder on: What is your dream/your deep "why"? What is your heart's burning desire? What problems can you help solve? What heartache have you endured that you can help another person not go through?

9

Secret Nine
The Power of S.M.A.R.T.E.R. Goal Setting

Now, we cannot talk about dreams and burning desires without talking about goal setting, as that's your GPS to your destiny.

Why should you set goals? Goal setting is like a life map. It is a powerful process that plays a fundamental role in designing how we want to experience our future, and it works as a fuel to develop skills and knowledge required to attain the end results we are aiming for. When you effectively set your goals, it helps you stay focused, holds you accountable, and is the single aspect of reaching your burning desires/dreams.

Having clear goals moves ideas to a reality. It motivates us, tells us where to concentrate based on what we want to achieve, and it also helps us flex our self-control muscles when temptations that could hinder our success come our way.

Can you imagine taking a road trip without a destination in mind? How will you know which turn to take when you don't even know where you are going? How will you know when you have reached your destination if you do not have one? That also means you will take any road that looks interesting, even without knowing where it leads, because you don't know where you are going anyway.

A lack of clearly defined and written goals is like sleepwalking. It is basically like going to a party where you aren't invited and don't know anyone there. You would feel out of place, right? I bet!

The best place to start is to ask yourself: What would be the one important thing that, if I accomplished by December next year, would make me feel successful? Identify it, write it down, visualize it, and meditate on it daily.

Setting goals is much more than just saying "I want to." Goal setting helps both to guide you, excite you, and hold you accountable. Remember, goals are different for everybody and differ depending on values, experiences, lifestyle, and the individual's definition of success. It really all comes down to what makes you happy, what impact you want to make, and what will make you feel complete/fulfilled.

Maybe you want a better job that gives you more time with your children. Or maybe it's baking and selling your favourite goodies to make extra cash to go on a vacation somewhere. Perhaps you want to become a renowned motivational speaker to motivate the masses. Your goal could be becoming a manager or high-ranking position at your job. It could also be to save money to buy your first home. Whatever your goal may be, keep it concise, simple, and clear and make sure it's something compelling and inspires you to wake up excited about it.

EIGHT SIMPLE STEPS TO SET GOALS

1. Brainstorm a list of everything you would like to achieve. Do not overthink it; just write whatever pops into your mind. This should not take you more than ten minutes.

2. Looking over your list, pick the first five that really speak to your heart, and give them a specific date you would like to achieve them by.

3. This is where the meat and gravy are! This is where you get to reveal your "why" -- your burning desire for your goal. In this section, be very specific to explain why you must achieve this goal, rain or shine, by the stated date. Ideally, set one for six months, one year, three years, five years, and ten years to start. Write a paragraph or at least more than five full sentences, minimum, for each goal.

4. Now that you have identified your goals, written them down, and dug deeper into why these goals are extremely important to you, we are going to condense them down. Nobody has time to read all those paragraphs twice a day, especially in the early rush hours. So, let's make them easy to read at a glance! (By the way, did you know that people do not read in words? If I tell you I have an iPhone 11 Pro, do you see the words iPhone 11 Pro or do you see a phone with Apple logo on it, three cameras, and a flat screen? I am not sure about what you saw when you read those words, but most people would see the phone features or the creator of apple. It's time to make your goals easy to see using pictures, just like we just did for Apple!) Look at magazines, Pinterest, and Google to find a picture that aligns with your goals. This is the only time you will hear me tell you I can see my future! If your goal is to have a mansion by the water, then find a picture that looks like it and print it out.

5. Hey! We are going shopping here! Head over to any store that sells poster boards, foam boards, or cork boards. Purchase whichever type and size you feel you will need. According to Wikipedia: "A dream board or vision board is a collage of images, pictures, and affirmations of one's dreams and desires, designed to serve as a source of inspiration and motivation, and to use the law of attraction to attain goals." This is exactly what you are going to make! While at the store, also grab tape, pins or glue (depending on which board you buy or how you want it to look), markers, pins, glue,

scissors (if you do not already have one) and some highlighters.

6. Time to become creative. In this step, bring your vision board to life! Cut up all the pictures you printed and tape, pin, or glue them onto the board. In addition to the pictures, I have empowering words (my affirmations) and empowering verses (for believers) on mine.

7. Act on your goals! It's fun and exciting doing all the above steps, but it's ultimately useless if you have it sitting there looking pretty and you are doing nothing about it. Start attaining the knowledge/skill required or start saving up for the funds you need in order to start that business or travel. You want to move forward with your vision, immediately.

8. Review/self-check. It's advisable to re-evaluate how you are doing, where you could improve, have you reached your goal, are you stuck and need to ask for support, etc. Take time to reflect honestly and kindly to yourself.

Do not complicate things. Keep them simple, detailed, and clear and have a blast! There is also a S.M.A.R.T.E.R. way to goal setting using some provoking questions that will help you as you plan, work, and execute your goals.

STEPS TO STRATEGICALLY SET GOALS USING S.M.A.R.T.E.R. METHOD

S- SPECIFIC: Be specific.

Being specific when setting up your goals enables you to see and understand your goals. If losing weight is your goal, then do not just write lose weight. Put a number of kgs/lbs and the date on it. This is also where you think of your what, why, who, when, where, and how.

What: what exactly do I want to accomplish?

Why: why is this goal important to me?

Who: who could help me achieve it?

When: when will I accomplish this by?

Where: where can I outsource the knowledge, skills required, or support?

How: how will I know when I have achieved my goal?

What: what are possible roadblocks and what will I do to overcome them?

M- MEANINGFUL: Make sure your goal is meaningful.

I am a personal-development junkie, and from the books I have read, the trainings I have attended, and the videos I have watched, you are more likely to hit your goal if it is something tangible, something emotional. It must be something deep and motivates you to the point you are willing to drop everything that does not serve you or leads you away from your goal. This includes some negative people and hobbies. This is tough.

A- ACHIEVABLE: The goal must be achievable/realistic.

I am a big believer in setting a bar high and that you can achieve whatever you put your mind and time into. However, as much as this is true, be realistic when setting goals, especially short-term ones. Again, the purpose of the goal setting is to motivate you, excite you, and keep you on course, which is why we put them on our board to view daily. They are not to exhaust you or discourage you. You can always set higher goals when you achieve the small ones, but make sure your goals are attainable within the specified time frame.

To help you on this step, ask yourself these questions:

Based on my current demands of life and the time frame I am giving myself for this goal: is it realistic? I say this because we can't be hyped about goal setting and forget the other important things in our lives. A single lady only having to worry about work and fun has more room and can stretch a little longer than a mother of a toddler, having to worry about childcare, and meeting his/her needs.

How will I accomplish this goal? It's great having a goal, but you gotta have a game plan.

R- RELEVANT: Your goal must be relevant to where you want to go in life.

You want to ensure the goals you are setting are aligning with what you want in your life, your core values, you career, etc. When your goals are aligned with your core values and directions in life, it helps keep you focused and consistent. You also want to make sure your goals marry each other and are not contradicting one another. This will help you in knocking them all down without losing control or sacrificing one for the other.

T- TIME-BOUND: Put the tag on it.

Put dates next to your goals. A goal without a target date, no matter how deep it might be, is just a wish. I say this because we use a word called tomorrow or next year and we sing that song until we get tired and forget. This is where we also prioritize our daily doings to make time for our goals.

It took me a year to get my life insurance license because, when I was studying for it, I kept saying I'm too tired or tomorrow, and the next thing I knew it was already a year later. I then told myself, "To hell with this business of 'tomorrow'!" I decided to get the license as a birthday gift to myself no matter what it took. After work, I would lock myself in my room and study for four hours with very few bathroom breaks, and in less than a month I was fully licensed. This step is a no-brainer if you are dead serious about your success in life. Even your boss and teachers know to give you deadlines on projects and assignments because they have mastered this step, consciously or not.

E- EVALUATE: Take time to reflect.

It is imperative that you ensure your daily activities are leading to your success. I do mine before bed when reflecting on my day to see what I did well and where I could improve tomorrow. It is good to evaluate at the halfway mark and celebrate! This motivates you to push even harder.

- What is going well?

- On a scale of one to ten, are my daily activities leading me toward achieving my goals?

- Where could I improve?

R- RE-ADJUST: Change gears, if needed.

Life happens, but if your goal is so important to you, then no matter how many times you fall you will rise.

- How consistent have I been with working on my goals?

- How satisfied am I with my results?

- Why did I do so well?

- What and why didn't I do so well?

- What can I change in terms of my approach and time management?

- Should I increase the bar since I am doing so well and feel excited about where my life is going, or do I need to break my goal into bit sizes to avoid feeling overwhelmed and increase the chances of reaching my goal with excitement?

Now, you have identified your dream and written it down, it's time to work towards them! It will require your full focus, your time, energy, a few tears, may require your money, and a lot of discipline, but trust me -- it's worth it!

As you take this step, please keep in mind that you may look crazy to some people, and you may get a lot of "no" from people, including your family. It may require you to step out of your comfort zone and even make some drastic changes to your lifestyle, but keep your eyes on the result. If it is truly your burning desire, then how badly do you want it? When feeling low or about to give up, go back to your deeper "why" and I promise that if it's big and burning enough, and you meditate on it daily, then no matter how many times you fall, you will get there. Always do your best and remember your best will not be the same every day. I am cheering for ya!

CONCLUSION

Sistergirl, thank you so much for taking a step towards becoming unstoppable and living the life you deserve. I hope you are immensely proud of yourself for taking a chance on yourself by investing both money and time in this book. If this book was gifted to you, please be sure to thank that person. Know that you matter to them, which is why they thought of you. Be proud of yourself and take time to celebrate this small, yet big, milestone! I am celebrating you!

Queen, *You Are a Damn Powerhouse* is much more than those listed titles or stories told throughout, and my aspiration is that you will shift your mindset and open yourself to receive and reclaim what is rightfully yours. It is your birthright to experience and live an abundant life. It is my heart's desire that you know this and hold it dear to your heart! My hope is that you have found this beautiful piece of art (book) beneficial and learned some practical tips on how to become unstoppable. My prayer is that you will know and understand that YOU ARE A DAMN POWERHOUSE, born fully loaded, and an original MASTERPIECE of God's own work. My desire is that you will OWN it, CLAIM it, and LIVE it out loud!

I invite you to start walking tall and intentionally taking up more space! I know you are probably thinking, *Well, isn't that being arrogant?* Beautiful, it is not! It's your world, just like it is for everyone else. So why walk with your shoulders hunched? Why should you hide yourself? After all, it ain't sexy anyways!

Sistergirl, I want you to pause for a moment. Put this book down and just visualize what your life would look like if you were free to fly like an eagle without worrying about what everyone else would think or say about you. I want you to visualize what your life would look like if you could have fun while enjoying parenting and not feel guilty about it. What would it feel like if you did what you love doing instead of dragging yourself to a job you hate so much? How would you feel if you did not feel obligated to say yes to everything, even against your will? What will you do about it and how soon?

What would it feel like to not carry all those grudges around on your shoulders anymore? What would a life of abundance look like to you? Beautiful, you deserve all the beautiful things the universe has to offer, and I want you to know that it is very much possible! It's all in you, my love!

No matter what you have been through, whether it be a nasty divorce, an early pregnancy, didn't go to school, bankruptcy, your partner left you for another woman, lost your job, or whatever other tragedies you have been through – you can heal from anything. I do not care where you have been. Sistergirl, I don't know what you have been through; it really doesn't matter, but I do know one thing: you are still a DAMN POWERHOUSE beyond measures. I want you to STAND in it, WALK it, and SLAY it regardless of what life has thrown at you.

Your past is in the past and *does not* define you nor does it determine your future. Sistergirl, I don't know very much English, but I damn know the difference between *being* and *been*! You are a human BEING, not a human BEEN. Your greatness lies within you and as long as you are still being (living), even the stars aren't a limit to your greatness!!

Girl, I also want you to know that whatever anyone else says or thinks about you is none of your business. What God or whatever higher being you believe in says -- that *is* your business! Whatever you feel like doing when you feel like doing it -- that is your business.

I stand in the gap for you if you can't stand in there for yourself yet, and I BELIEVE IN YOU! Sister friend, I salute you. I am here to hold your hand and walk the journey with you. From another single mama's heart to yours. Always remember that you are a limitless powerhouse!

I will leave you with a quote one of my mentors posted on her social media as I was wrapping up this book, and it really resonated with me, especially during this pandemic.

> To dare to dream in the midst of adversity, in the midst of failure, in the midst of complacency, is to have hope. That hope, that dream, is a gift from God. It is His way of telling you that He has a plan for your life if you will listen and give Him a chance to bring it to pass. I believe with all my heart that each one of us has been given unique gifts from our Creator and that each of us is called to apply those gifts to a purpose in life.
>
> -Dani Johnson

I have just put down my ink and I invite you to do something!

Believe it or not, I literally started two businesses while writing this book (during a pandemic, while moving up and down, while finishing my book in the student dorm with just a bathroom and a very small kitchen, all while sharing a bed with my daughter in the night and using our bedroom as an office during the day). From here I contacted all the amazing ladies who contributed to this book and where I did many coaching sessions, as well as dealing with potential business partners. I want to help women and single mothers explore and create their opportunities to dream big while they stay home with their children, or as a support in creating a side hustle to supplement their income. Girl, long gone are those days where people depended on one stream of income.

Please visit our website at www.youareadamnpowerhouse.com for inspirational blogs, T-shirts, and the best waist trainers!

While you are there, grab your FREE 30-minute coaching session with me and start your healing journey today! Let's discuss healing, mindset shifts, and how we can bring your heart desires to life!

And you can also shoot us an email for more information and how you can work with me at youareadamnpowerhouse@gmail.com.

I bid you well as your sister in strength and partner on the journey to the freedom land as we recycle our pain into purpose!

Cheers!

END NOTES

Preface

Vanzant, Iyanla. Acts Of Faith: Daily Meditations for People of Colour *(pg.9, January 1)*.

Healthy Babies Healthy Children, Region of Waterloo Public Health https://www.regionofwaterloo.ca/en/public-health-and-emergency-services.aspx

Chapter 2

Proverbs 18:21 NIV

John 1:1 NIV

Genesis 1:3 NIV

Vanzant, Iyanla. Acts Of Faith: Daily Meditations for People of Colour (pg. 168).

Schweitzer, Albert. https://www.brainyquote.com/quotes/albert_schweitzer_402282

Bonus Secret: Glenda Standeven

Angelou, Maya. "Let gratitude be the pillow upon which you kneel to say your nightly prayer. And let faith be the bridge you build to overcome evil and welcome good." https://www.azquotes.com

Chapter 3

Nichols, Lisa. "So often we take care of everybody and the whole time we're putting ourselves on the back burner. This is the season to 'do you' first." Facebook post on Lisa's main page. March 1st, 2018, 5:06 AM. https://www.motivatingthemasses.com

Unknown. A study into the everyday lives of 2,000 moms and dads. New York Post https://nypost.com/2018/10/03/parents-get-way-less-than-an-hour-per-day-of-me-time/

Dr. Aimee L. Danielson, PhD, a licensed clinical psychologist with specialized training and over 15 years of experience in Maternal Mental Health, a director of the Women's Mental Health Program at MedStar Georgetown University Hospital. https://www.medstargeorgetown.org/our-services/psychiatry/treatments/womens-mental-health/

Ruiz, Don. The Four Agreements. (6)

Chapter 4

Unknown. https://en.wikipedia.org/wiki/St._Joseph_Island_(Ontario)

Chapter 6

Sharma, Robin. "All change is hard at first, messy in the middle and gorgeous at the end." The 5 AM Club: Own Your Morning. Elevate Your Life. https://www.goodreads.com/

Chapter 7

Winfrey, Oprah. The more you praise and celebrate your life, the more there is in life to celebrate. https://www.brainyquote.com/

Bonus Secret: The Power of Giving

Vanzant, Iyanla. Acts Of Faith: Daily Meditations for People of Colour (pg 90). One Woman Foundation. https://onewoman.ca/

Chapter 8

Habakkuk 2:2 CEV
Proverbs 29:18 KJV
CNN Africa: https://www.cnn.com/2020/06/15/africa/ibidun-ighodalo-dead-nigeria/index.html
Ibidunni Ighodalo Foundation. https://ibidunniighodalofoundation.org/about-us/

Chapter 9

Wikipedia, the free encyclopaedia: https://en.wikipedia.org/wiki/Dream_board

Conclusion

Johnson, Dani. https://danijohnson.com

CONTRIBUTORS

BETTY JOHNSON is the founder of the Betty Ogiel Foundation, an author of the award-winning book *Against All Odds*: *Memoirs of Resilience, Determination and Luck Amidst Hardship for an African Girl Child in Her Passionate Pursuit for Education*. Ogiel is also an inspirational speaker whose mission is to inspire hope and transform lives. She is also a certified independence coach with the John Maxwell Team and a Human Resource Excellence Award as well as Peacemaker Award recipient.

JENNIFER RAMIREZ is the founder and executive director of & Rise., a non-profit organization that helps women become the ultimate versions of themselves through community and a sisterhood of like-minded women.

SABRINA RUNBECK is a Cardiothoracic surgery PA, a public health practitioner, and a peak performance coach/speaker who empowers ambitious young professionals, especially those working in healthcare, to become confident leaders. Her mission is to support these people so they can be BOTH a powerhouse in their career and feel passionate about life again without feeling overwhelmed, underappreciated, or undervalued.

GLENDA STANDEVEN is a hemi-pelvectomy amputee and award-winning inspirational speaker. She is the author of *What Men Won't Talk About and Women Need to Know: A Woman's Perspective on Prostate Cancer* and her autobiography titled *I Am Choosing to Smile.*

ABOUT THE AUTHOR

REBECCA MUTETE is a proud single mother of three amazing children. She was born and raised in the beautiful continent of Africa until she was sixteen years old when she immigrated to Canada while pregnant with her firstborn. As a high school dropout and a teen mom carrying lots of anger and resentment, Rebecca wasn't always driven and certainly wasn't always positive or enthusiastic about life. As she grew up and made her own wings to fly through life, she became unstoppable. Rebecca is on a mission to inspire, uplift, and help women transform and rediscover their inner-strength. Rebecca's dream is to see more women step out boldly and powerfully and embrace their God-given, unlimited potential. Rebecca believes that every woman -- no matter their background, their marital status, their educational levels, or whatever people consider "class" -- are powerhouses in their unique ways. She is now an author, life coach, and inspirational speaker. Visit www.youareadamnpowerhouse.com for more information.